"Global Doodle Gems" Flower Collection Volume 2

Drawn & colored by Nancy 43

Published "GDG" Global Doodle Gems

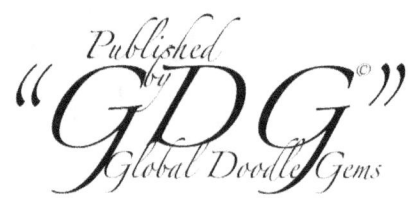

Share your colored versions with us ! We love seeing your results and hearing from you we are social !

The Official FB book page, stay on top of what we have in the works !
www.facebook.com/globaldoodlegems

The Community group, share your colored pages, meet the artists, enjoy exclusive freebies, take part in community Charity books and so much more......
www.facebook.com/groups/globaldoodlegems/

Follow us on Twitter.... @GlobalDoodlegem

We are on Instagram too
@globaldoodlegems for instagram

...and if you are not social like that we have a blog
globaldoodlegems.wordpress.com

Copyright © 2015 Global Doodle Gems

All rights are reserved by Global Doodle Gems.

Duplication of pages for personal use are allowed. You are invited to color the pages then scan/post your coloured versions to social networks, mentioning the book title and author/artist (Global Doodle Gems).

All artwork and images are protected by copyright laws. This book or any portion thereof may not, otherwise, be reproduced and/or distributed or transmitted without the express written permission of the artist/publisher of Global Doodle Gems.

All of us from the Global Doodle Gems wish you a colortastic time and look forward to seeing your wonderful color results online !

Participating Artists

1. Lilan Chen
2. Mireille W.
3. Nancy43
4. Nadège Zenfeerie
5. Rover Hsiao
6. Leaf Yeh
7. Neeti Goswami
8. Yaya
9. Johanna Ans
10. Ellen Wolters
11. Adriana Graciela Volpe
12. Alfred E. Villanueva
13. Maud Feral Chauveau (MFC)
14. Maud Taron
15. Isa Humeau

Contributing Artist
Lilan Chen
Taiwan

Facebook : lilanchen.art

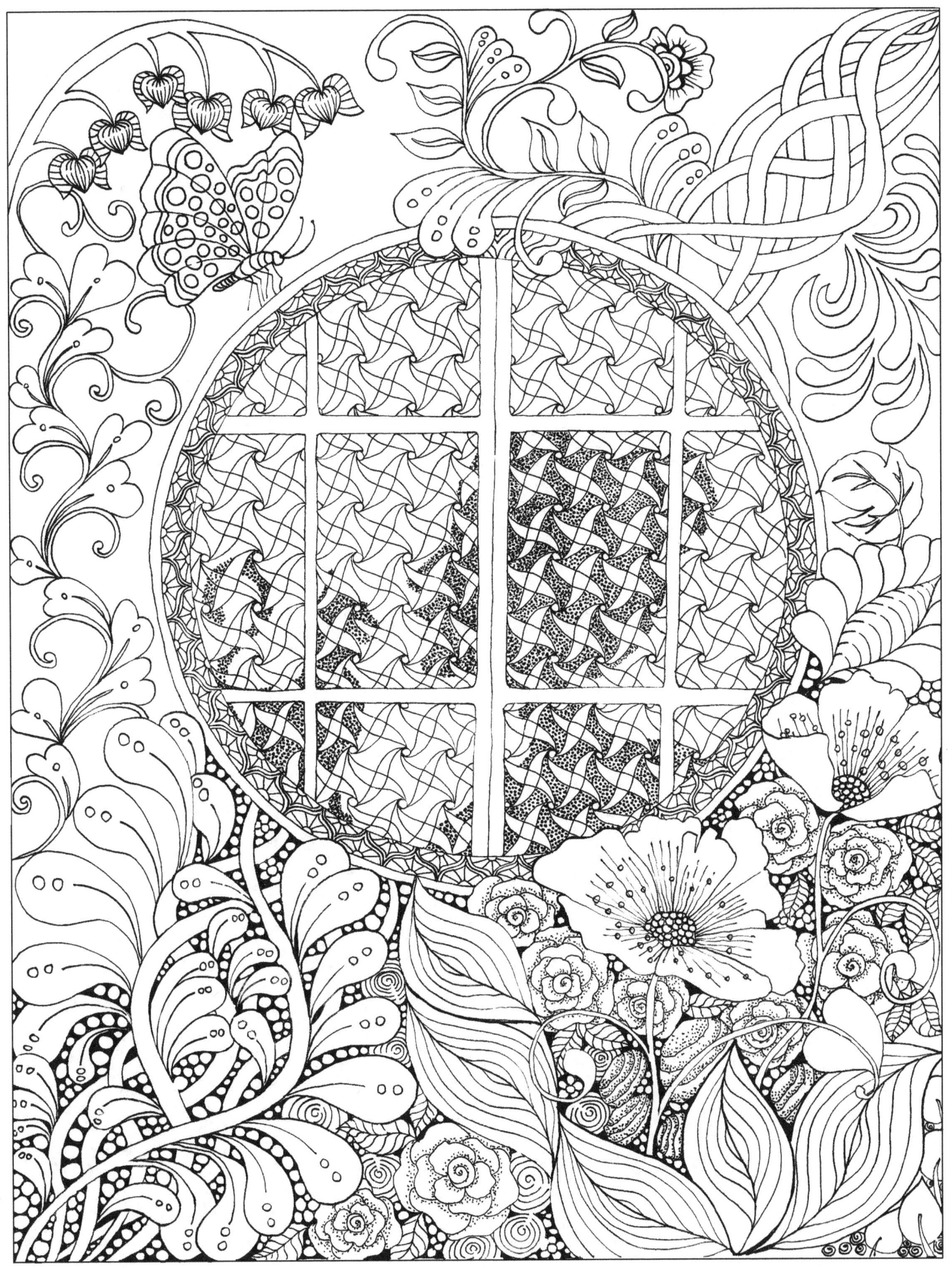

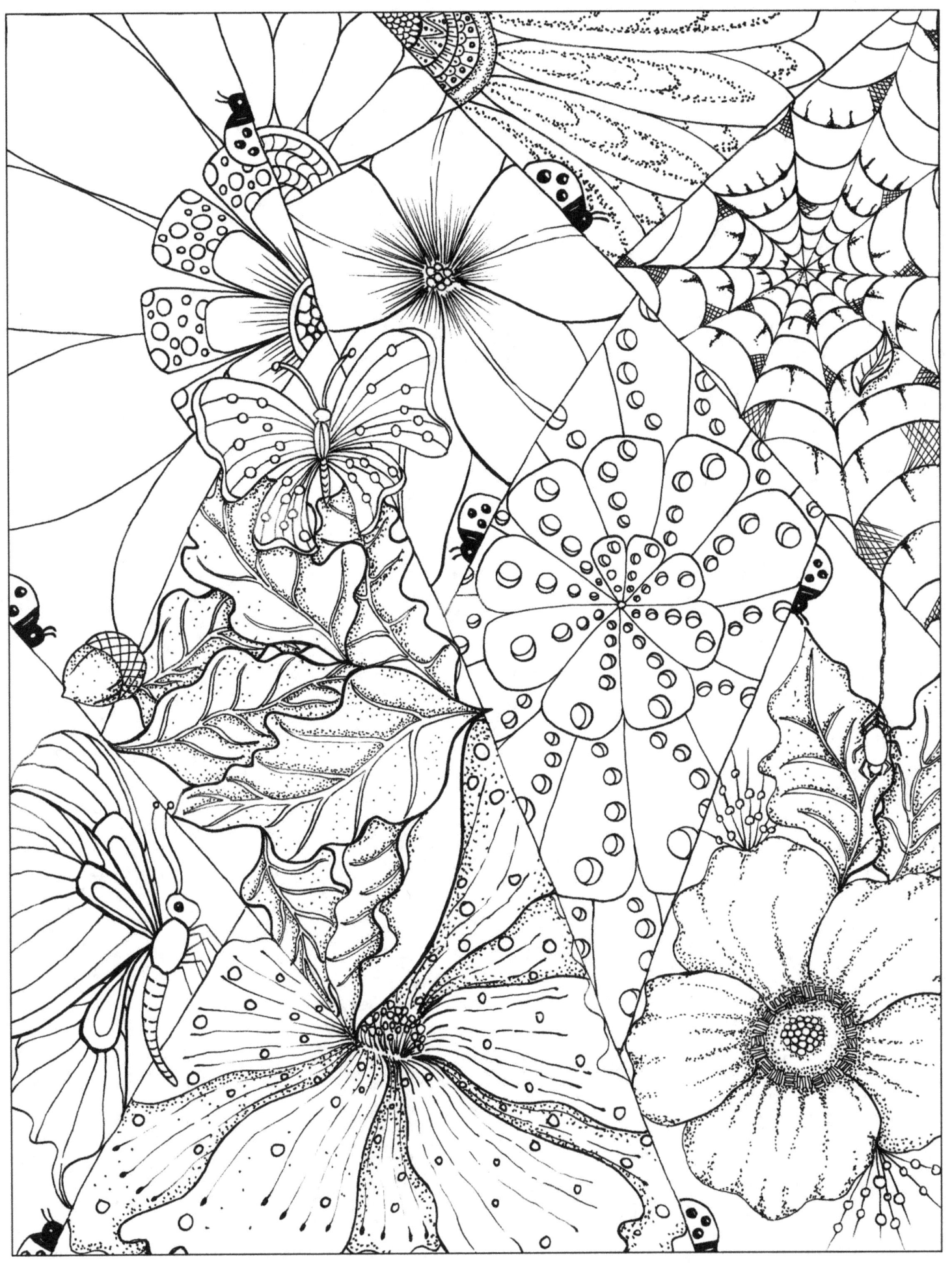

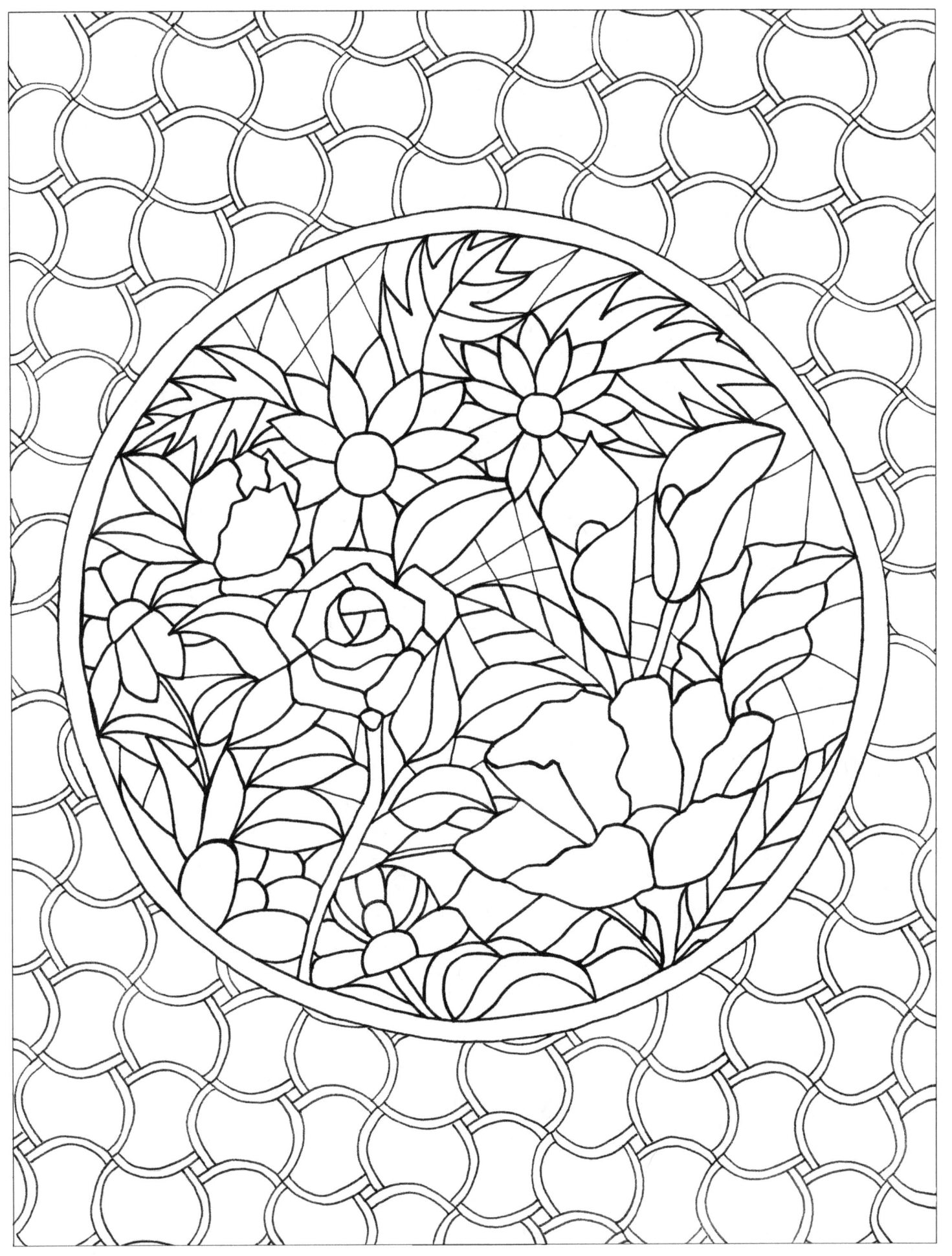

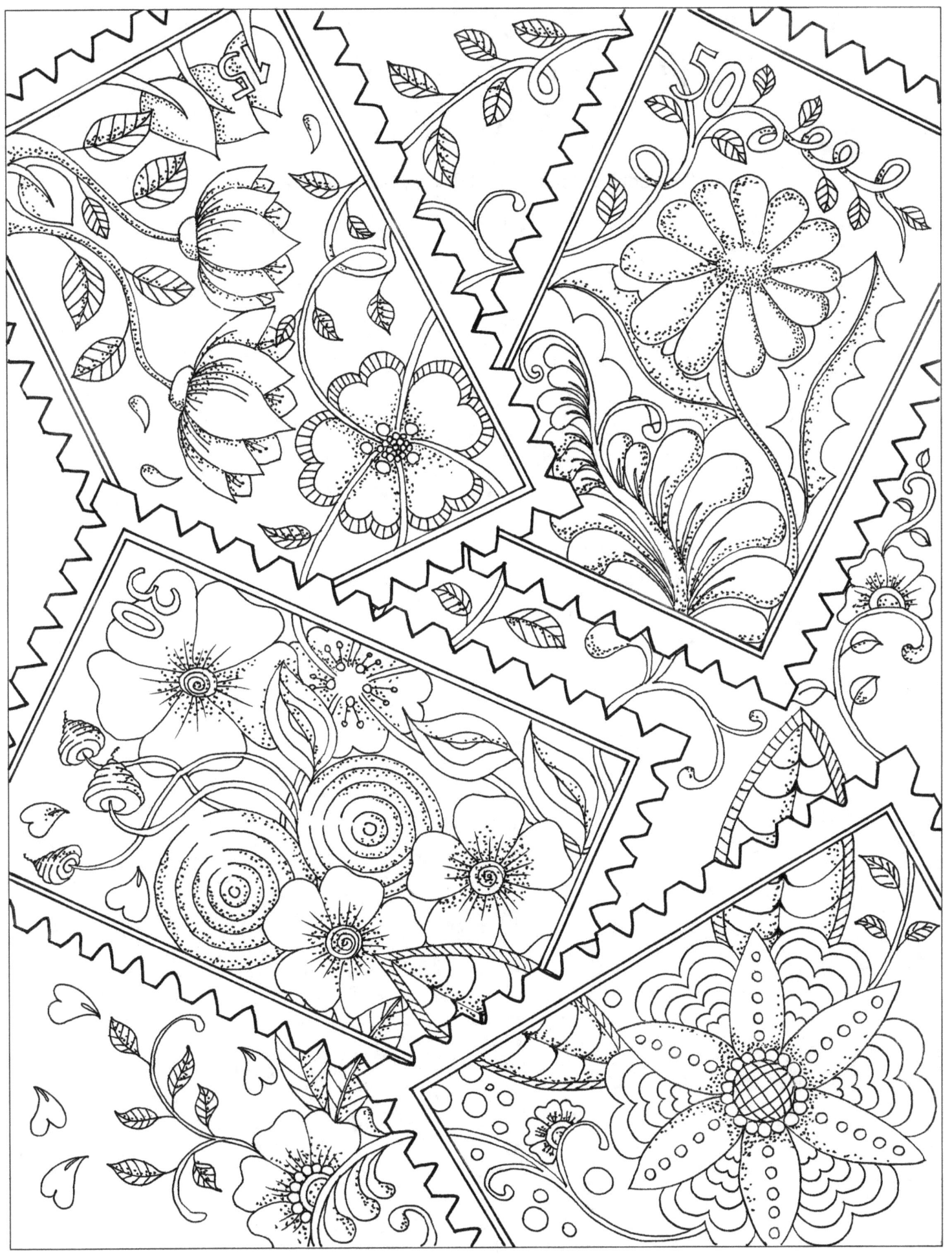

Contributing Artist
Mireille Westerduin, Colour by Mi
The Netherlands

Facebook : Colour-by-Mi-Kleurplaten-Illustraties

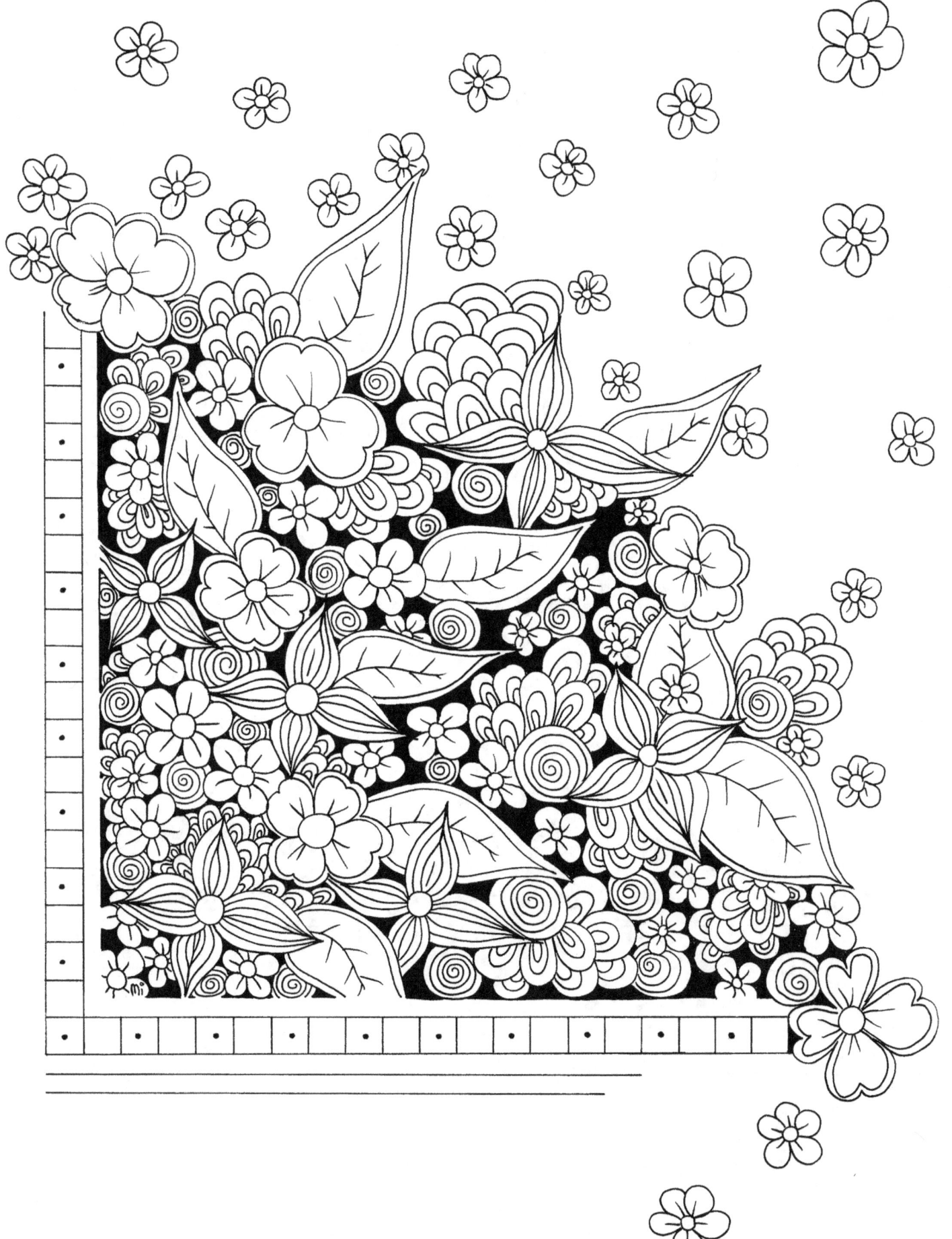

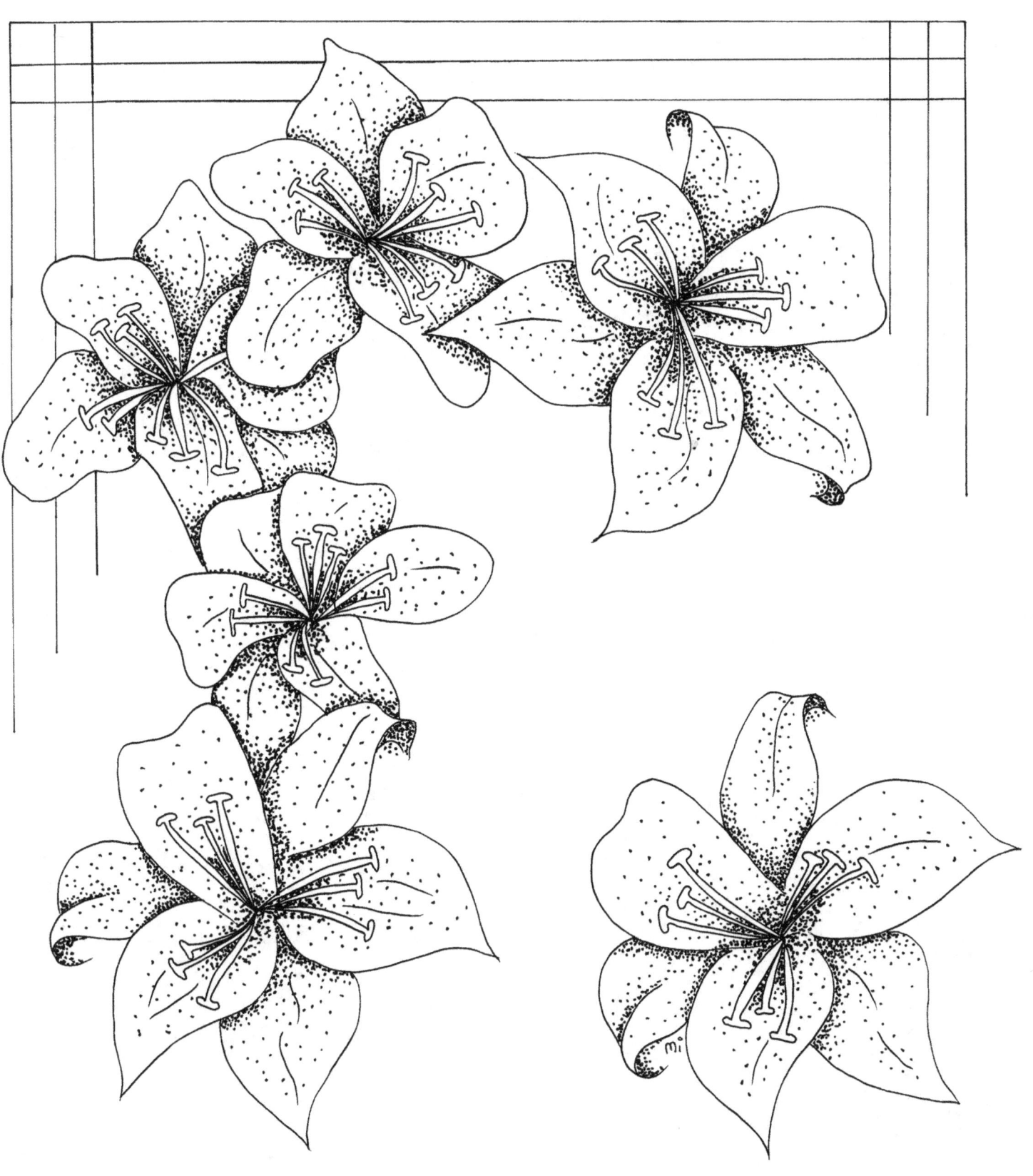

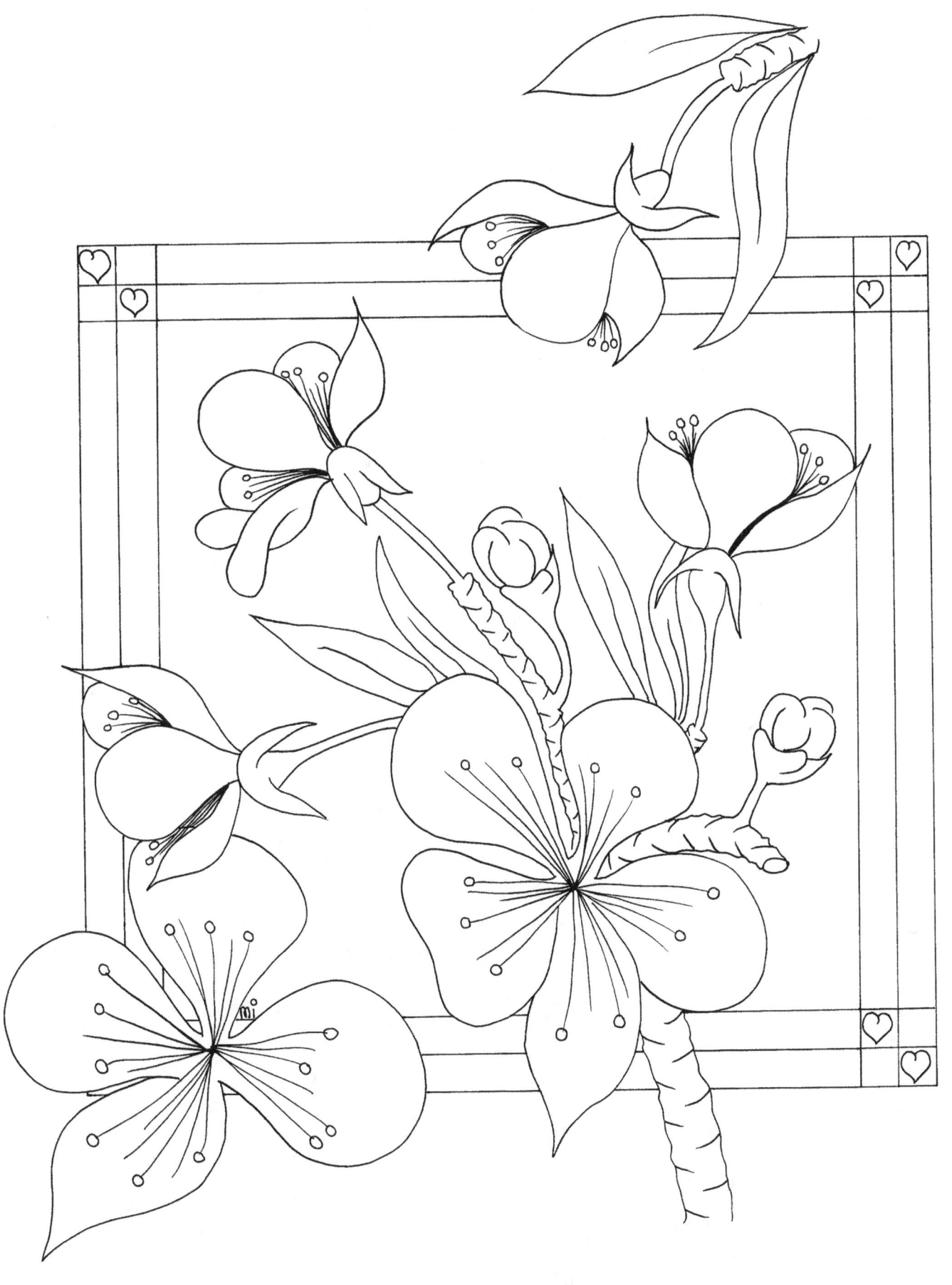

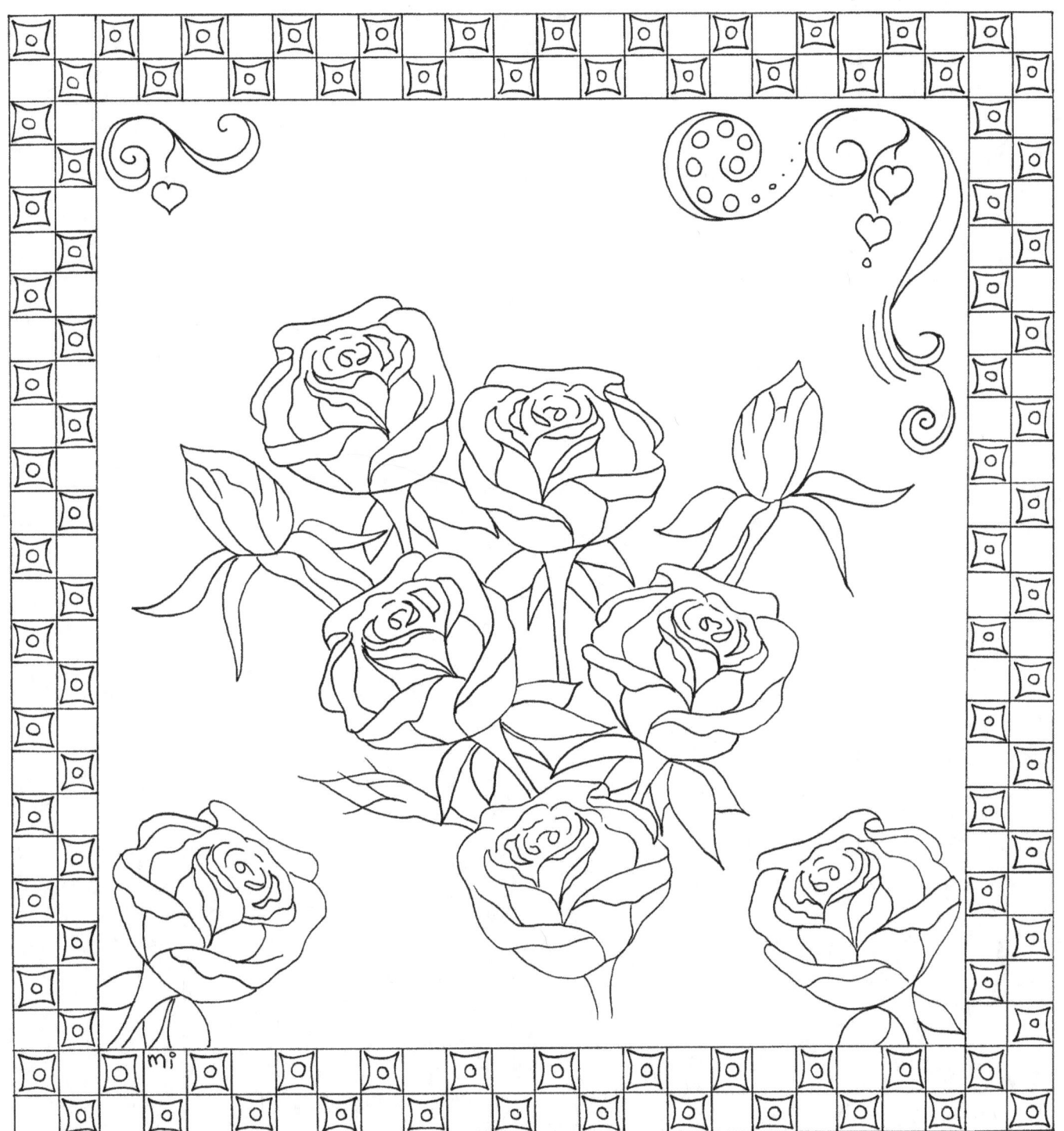

Contributing Artist
Nancy43
Taiwan

Facebook : 43Nancy43

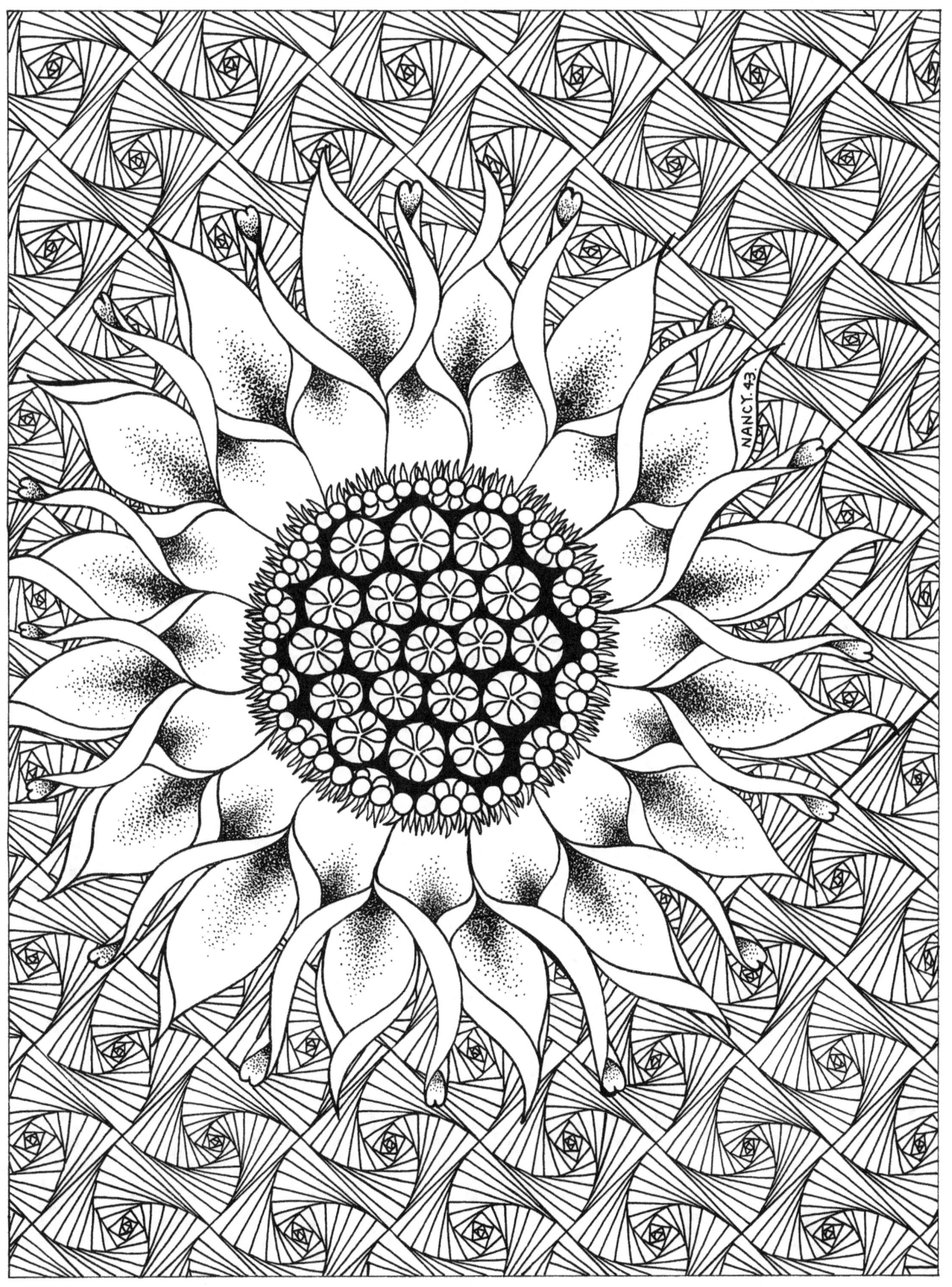

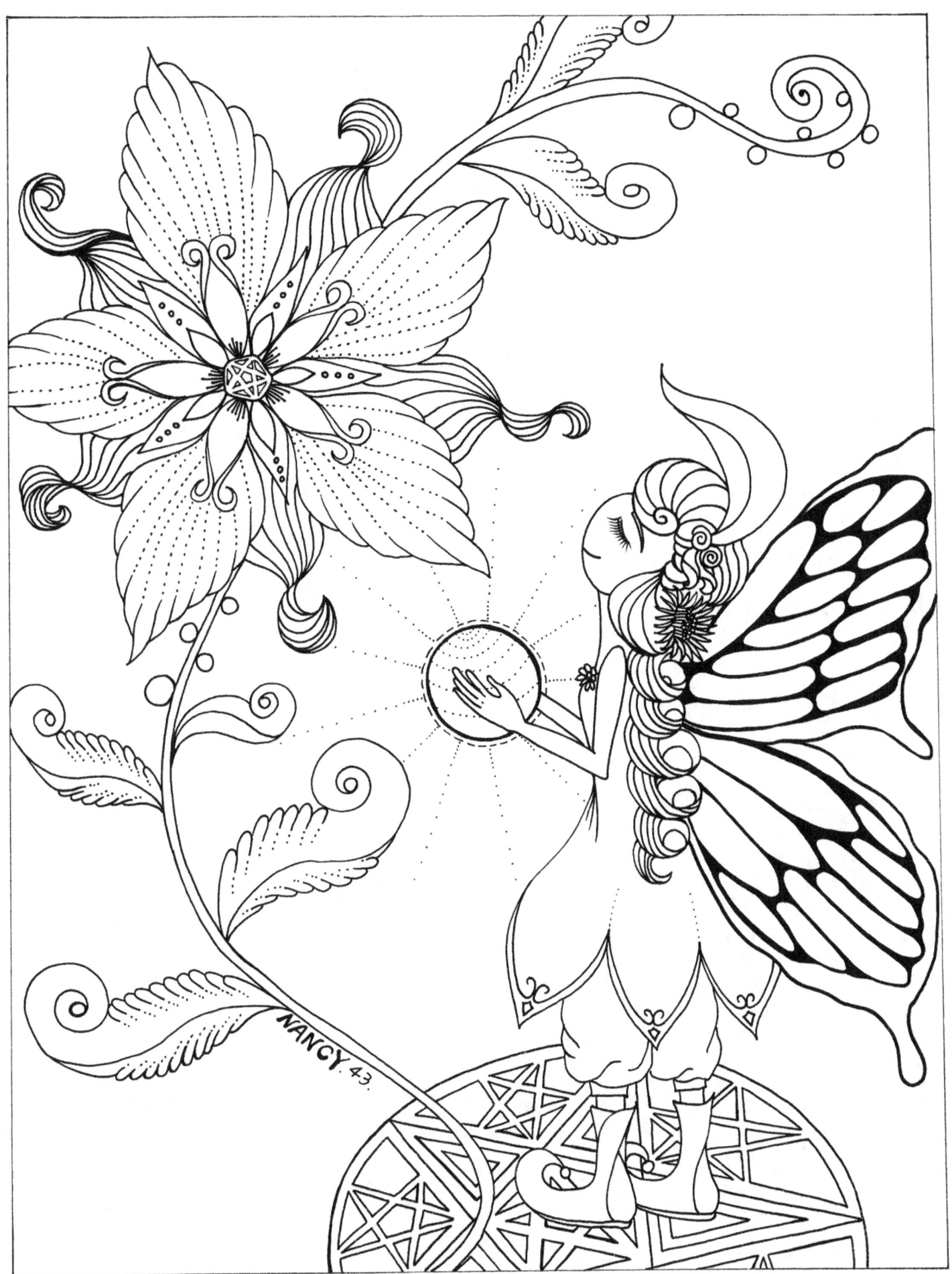

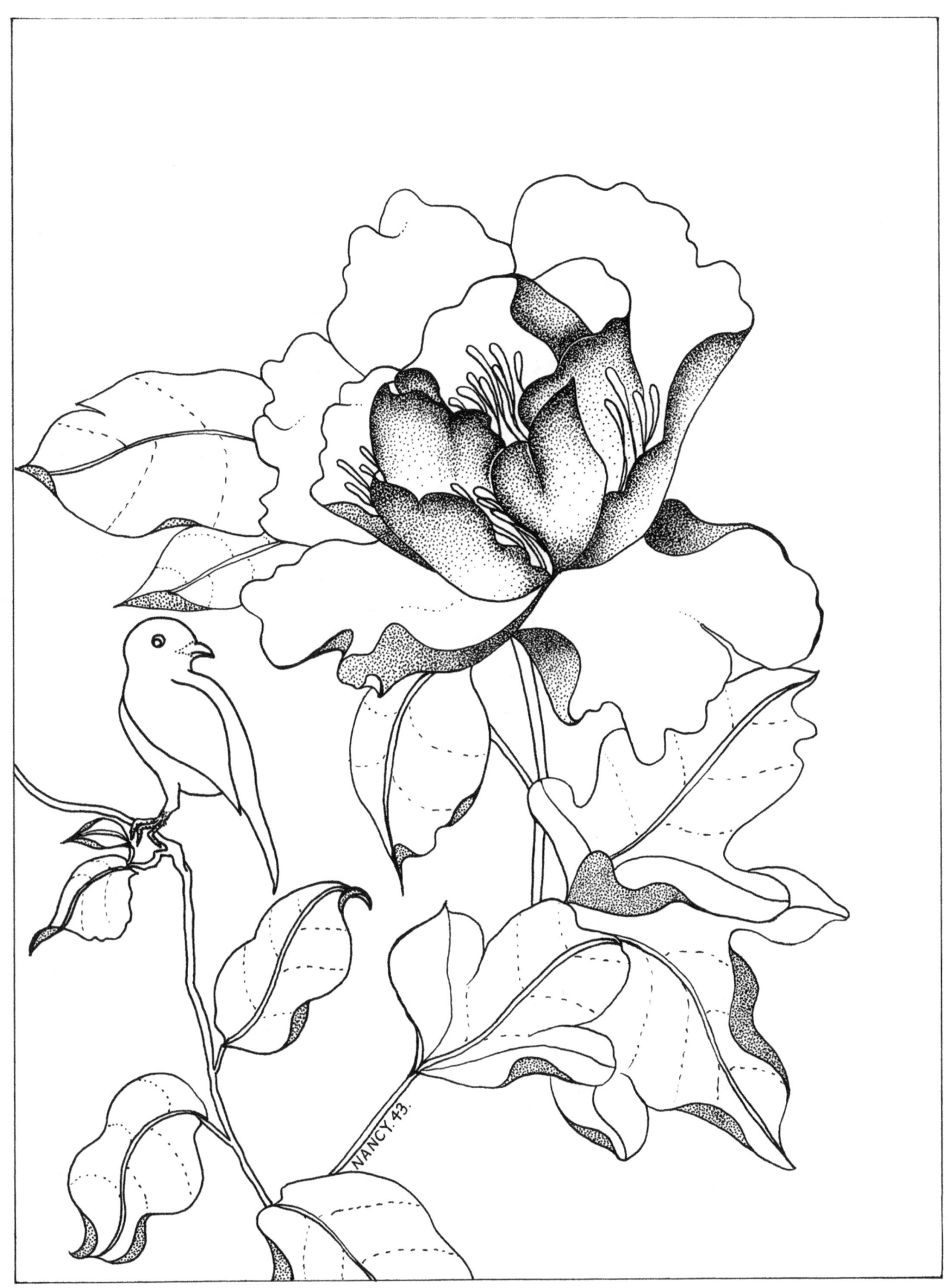

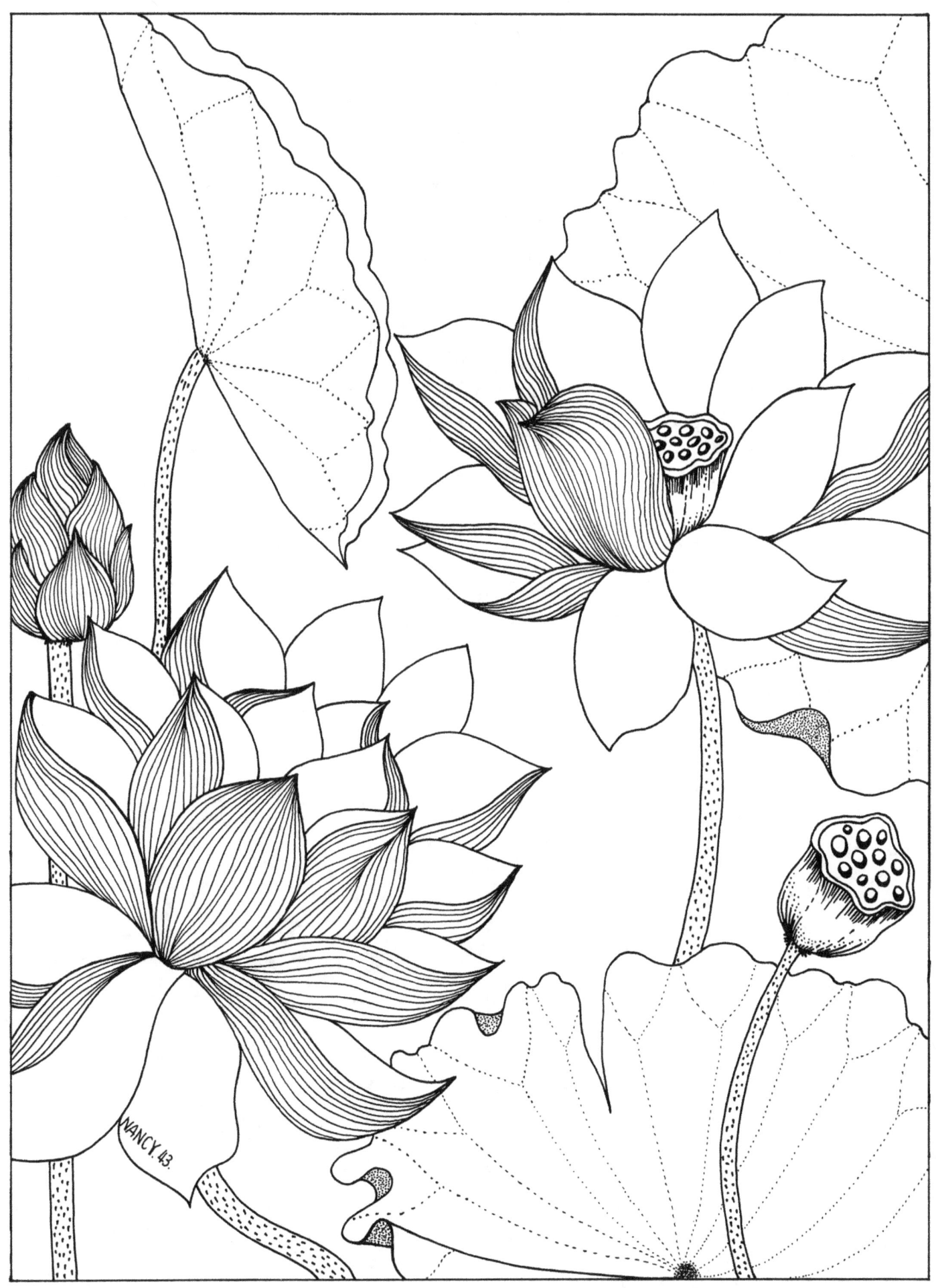

Contributing Artist
Nadège Zenfeerie
France

Facebook : zenfeerie

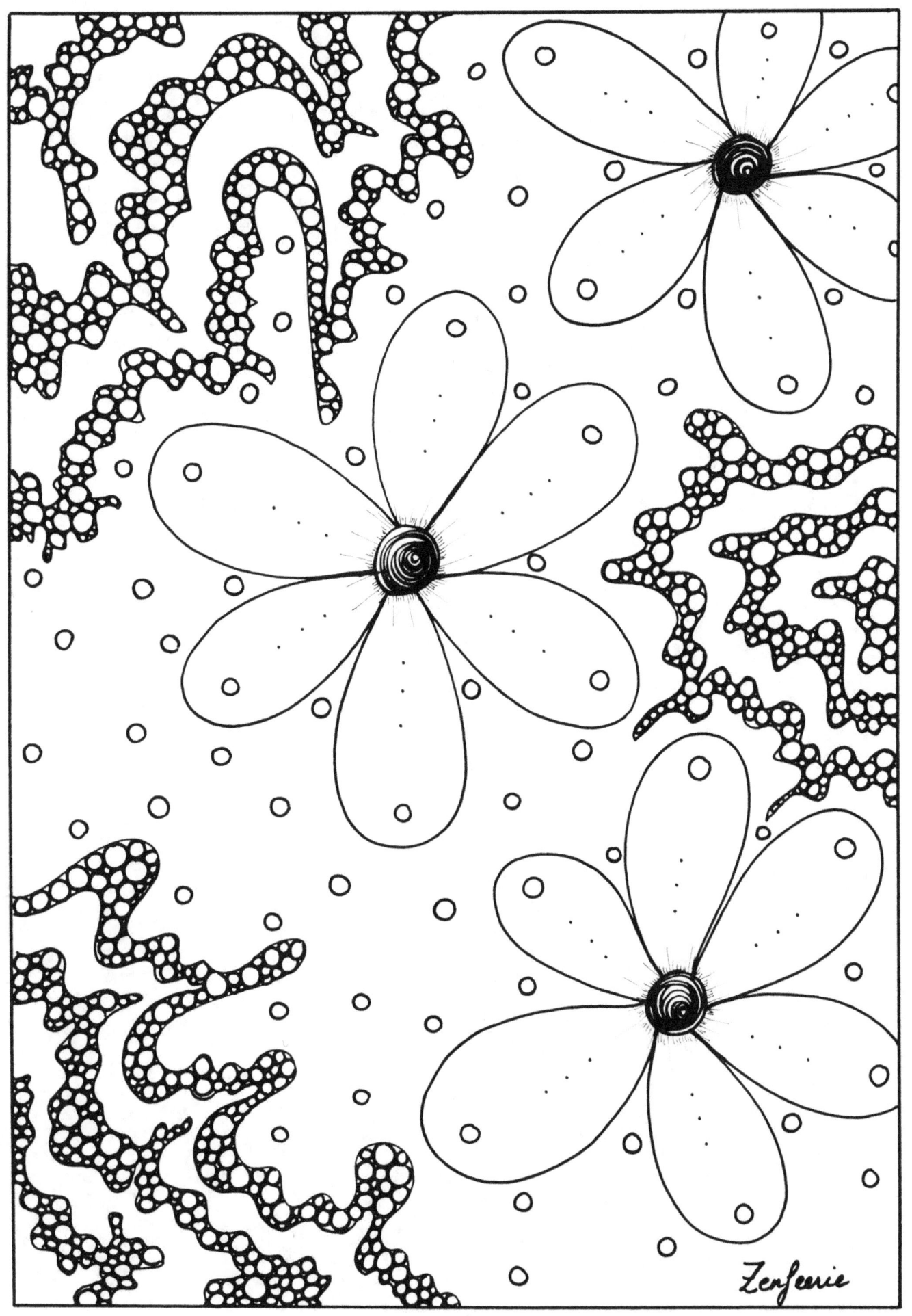

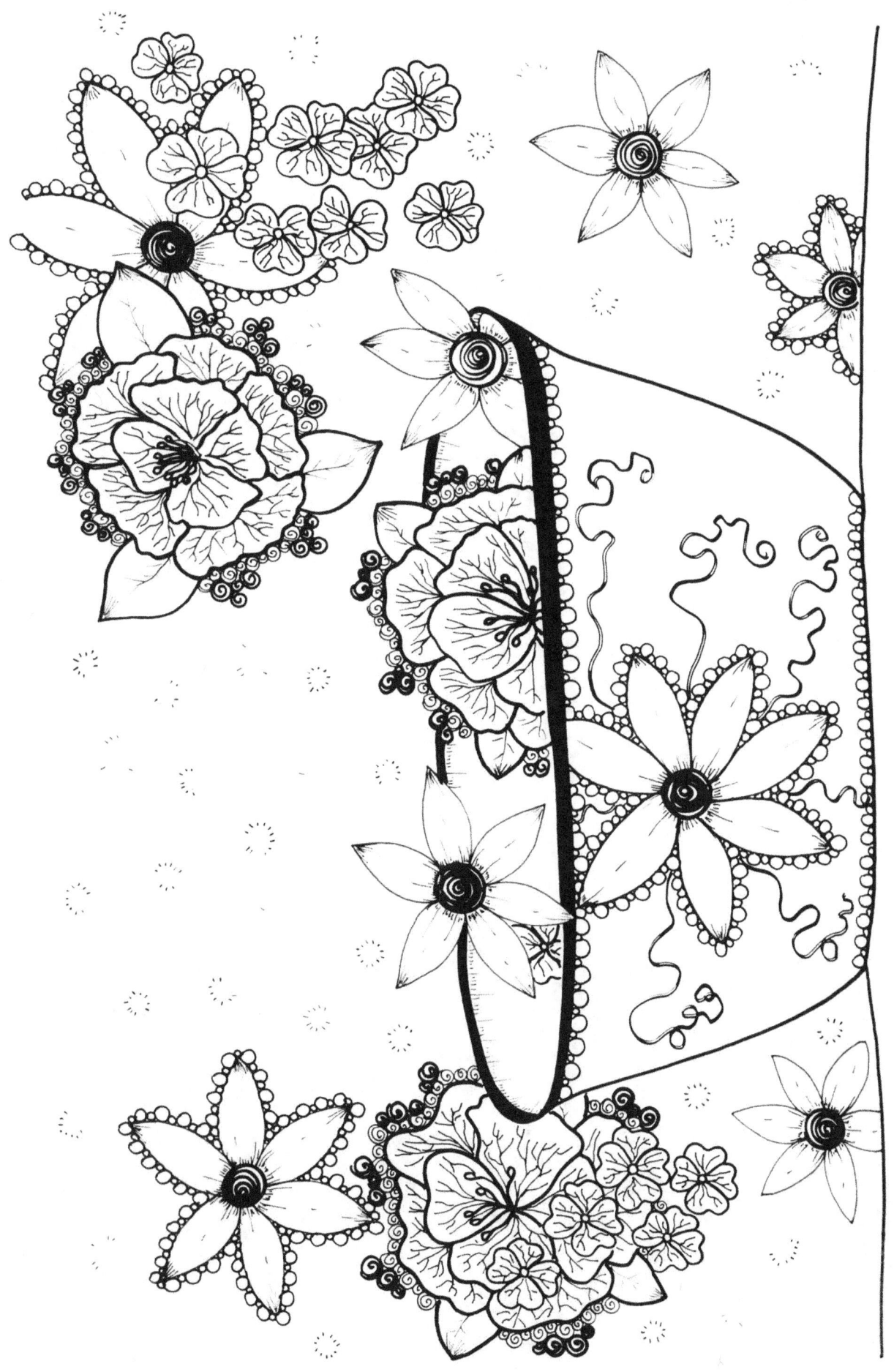

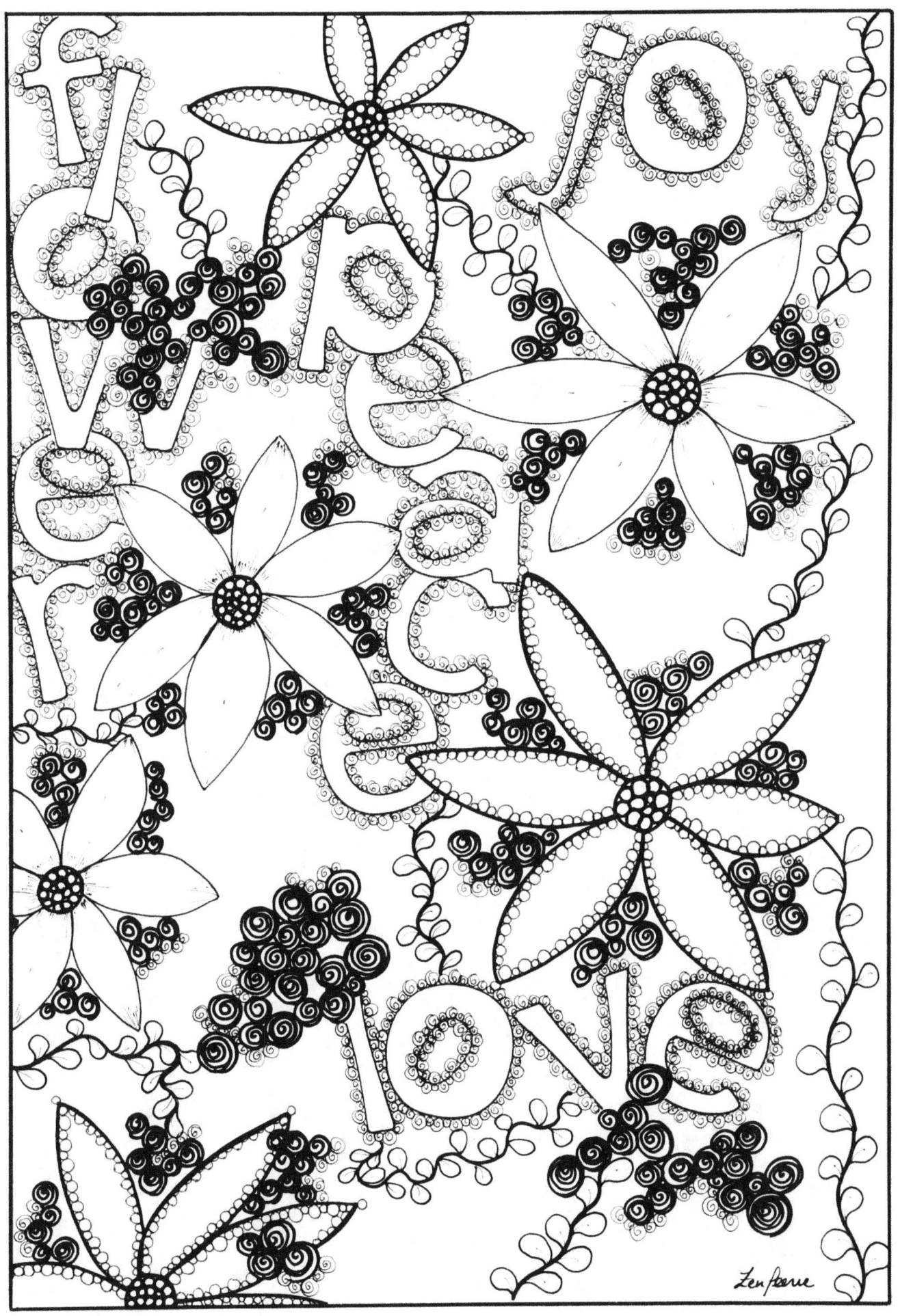

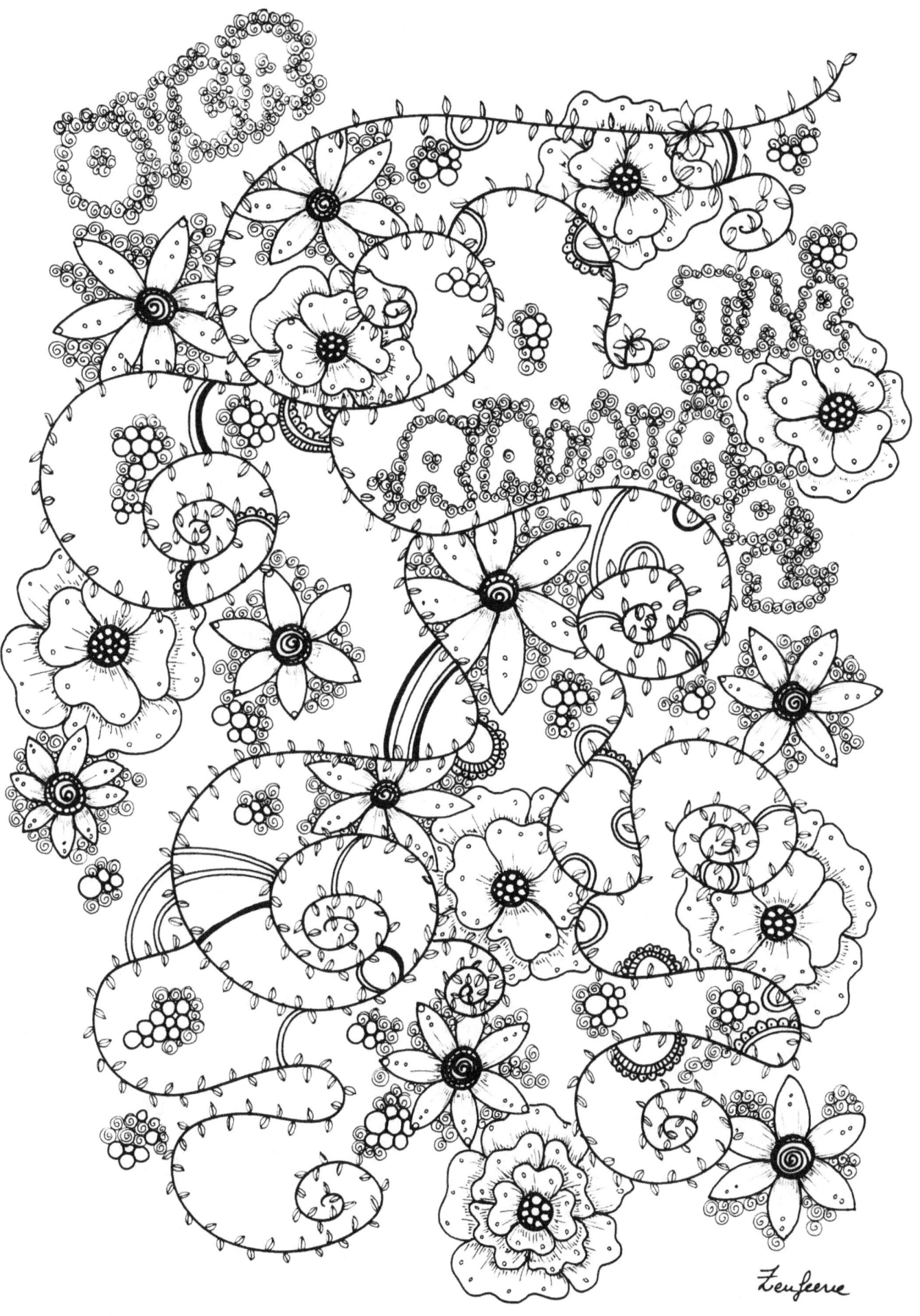

Contributing Artist
Rover Hsiao
Taiwan

Facebook : roverhsiao2015

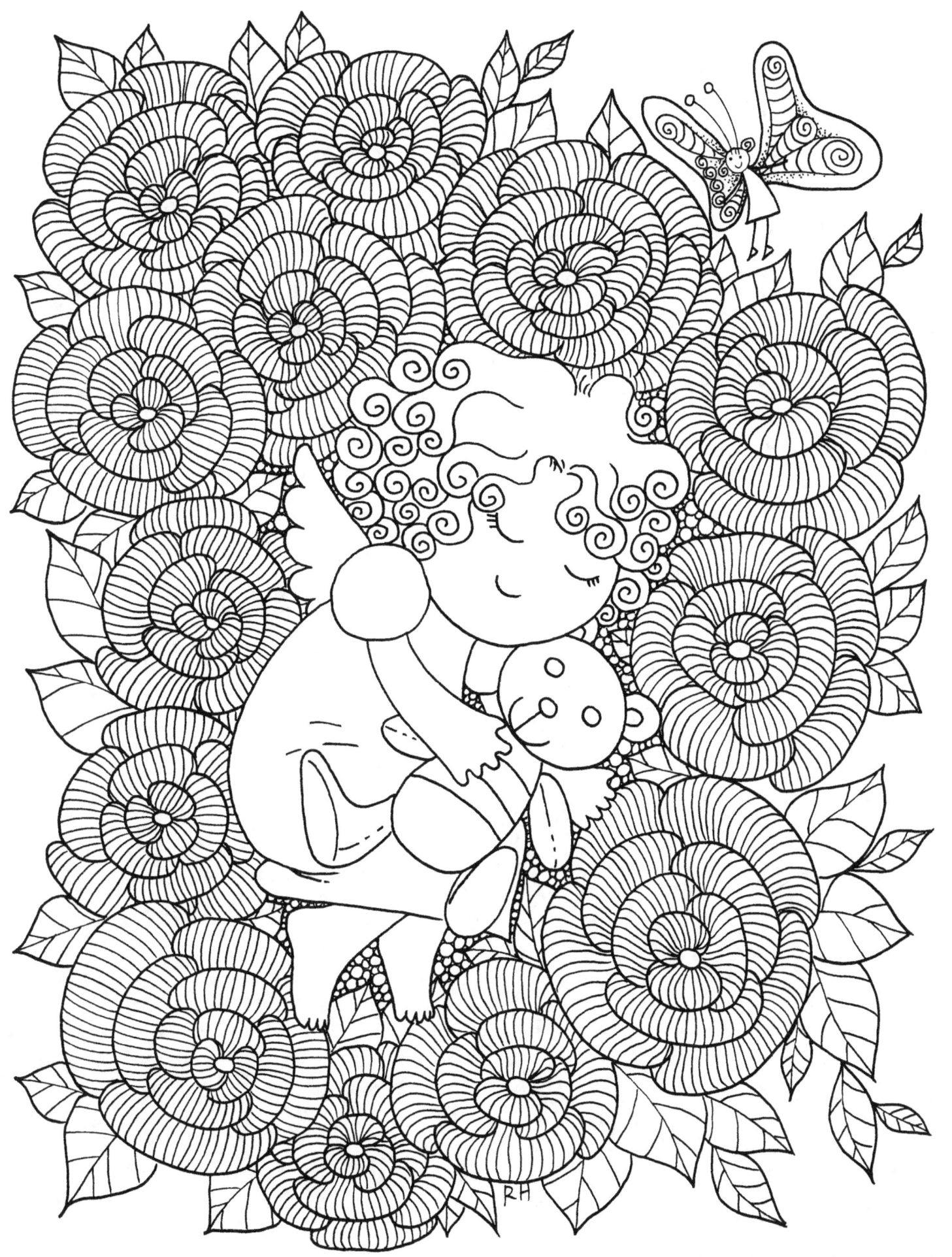

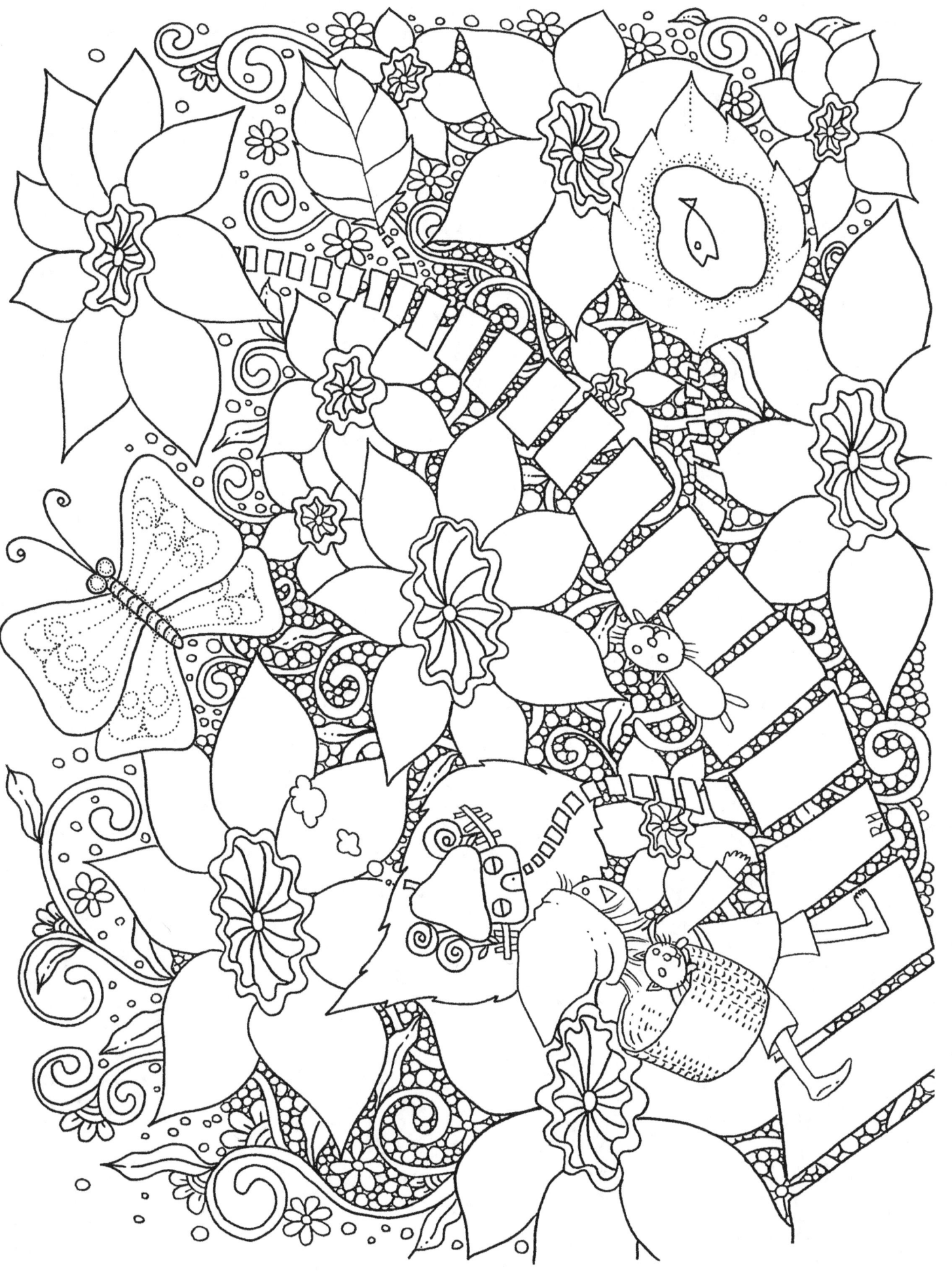

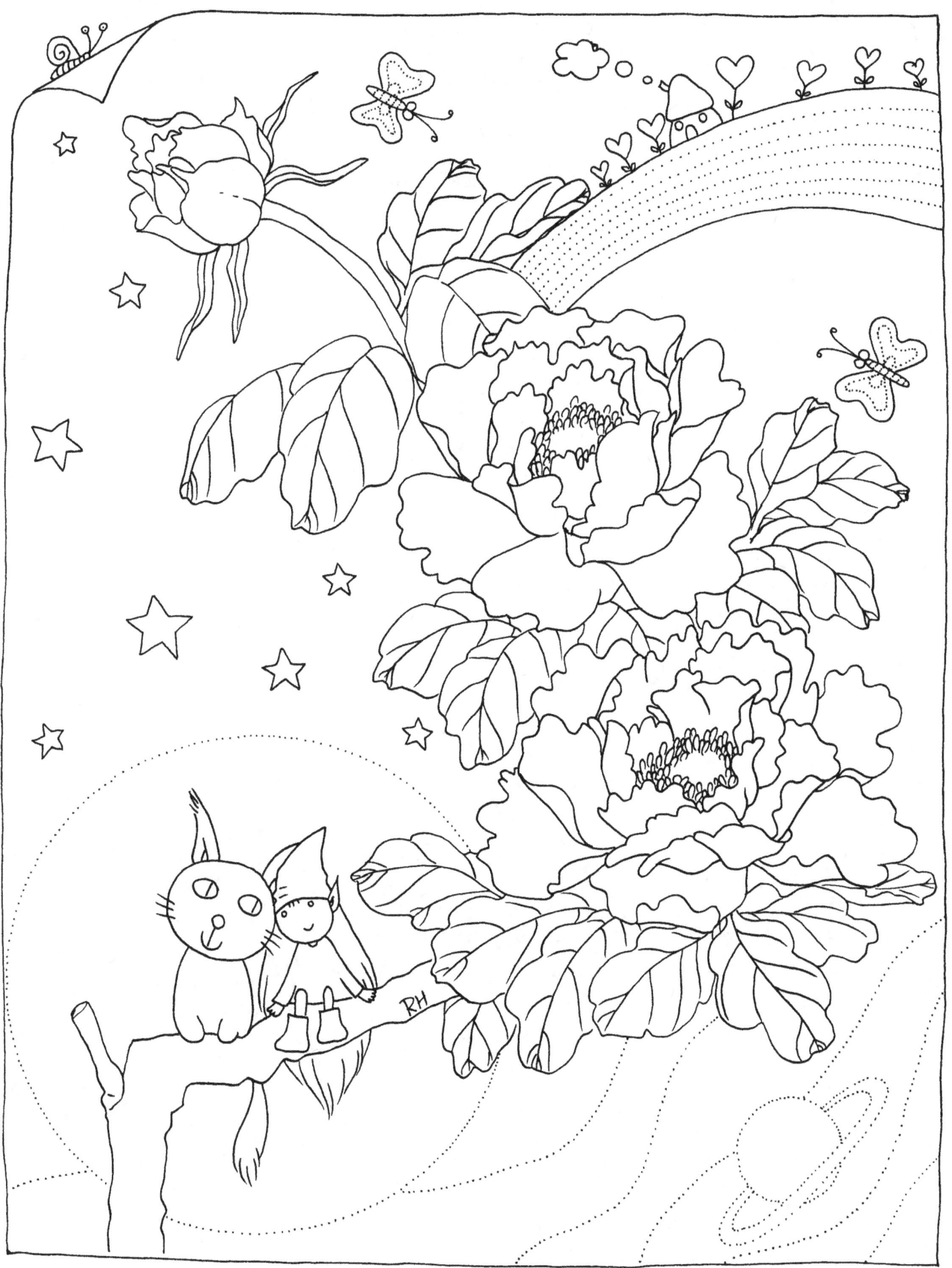

Contributing Artist
Leaf Yeh
Taiwan

Facebook : leaf.Painting

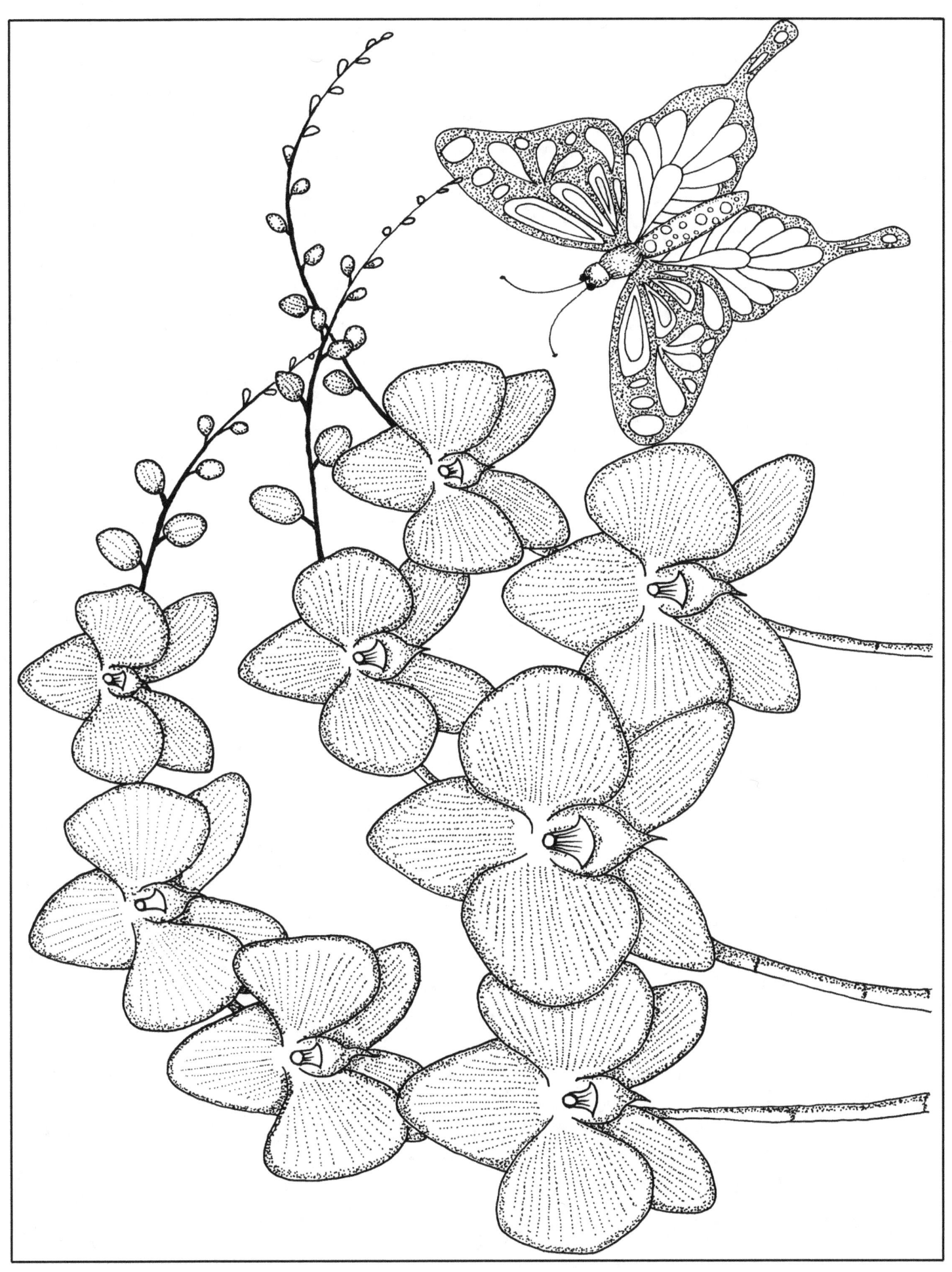

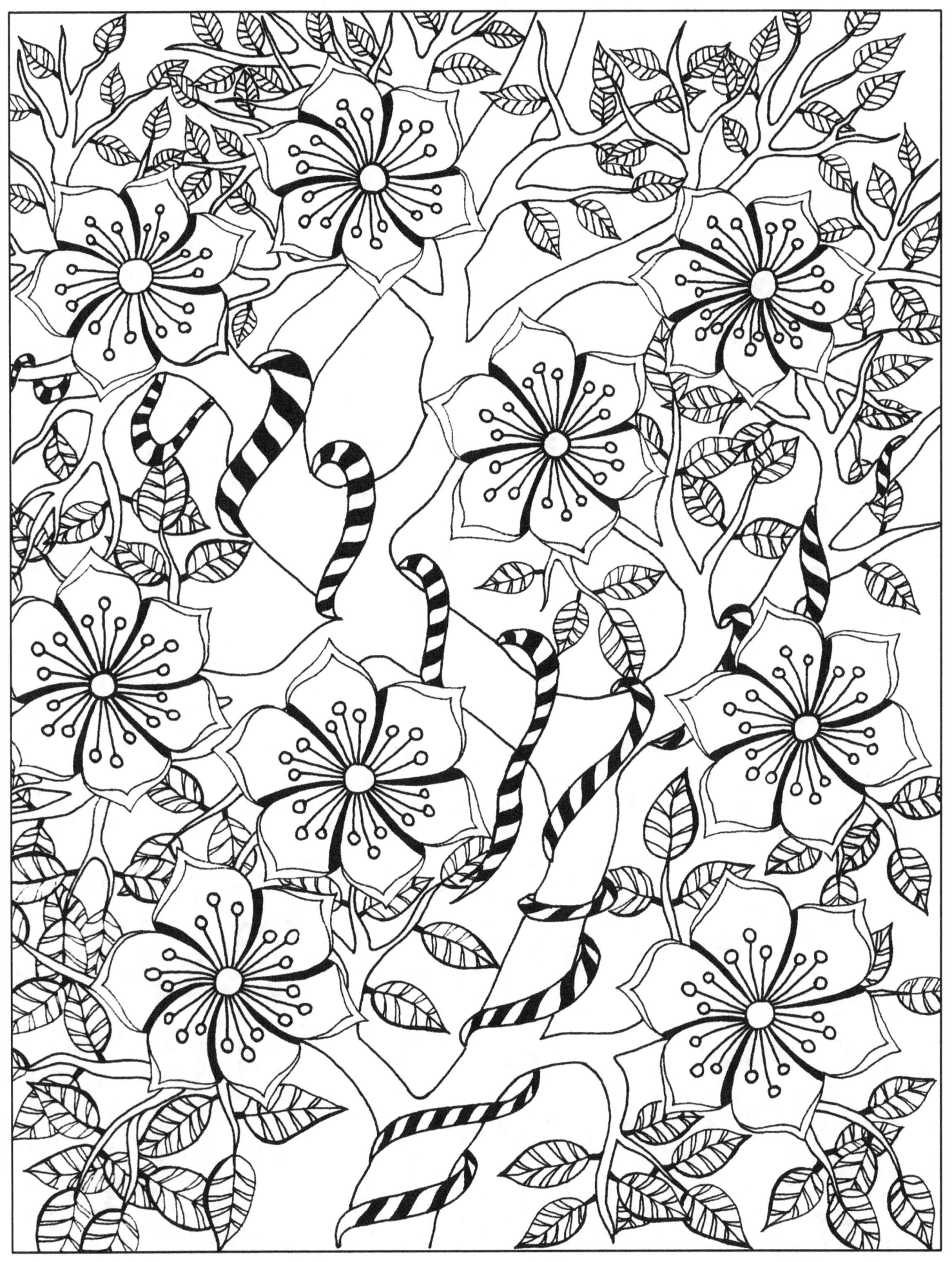

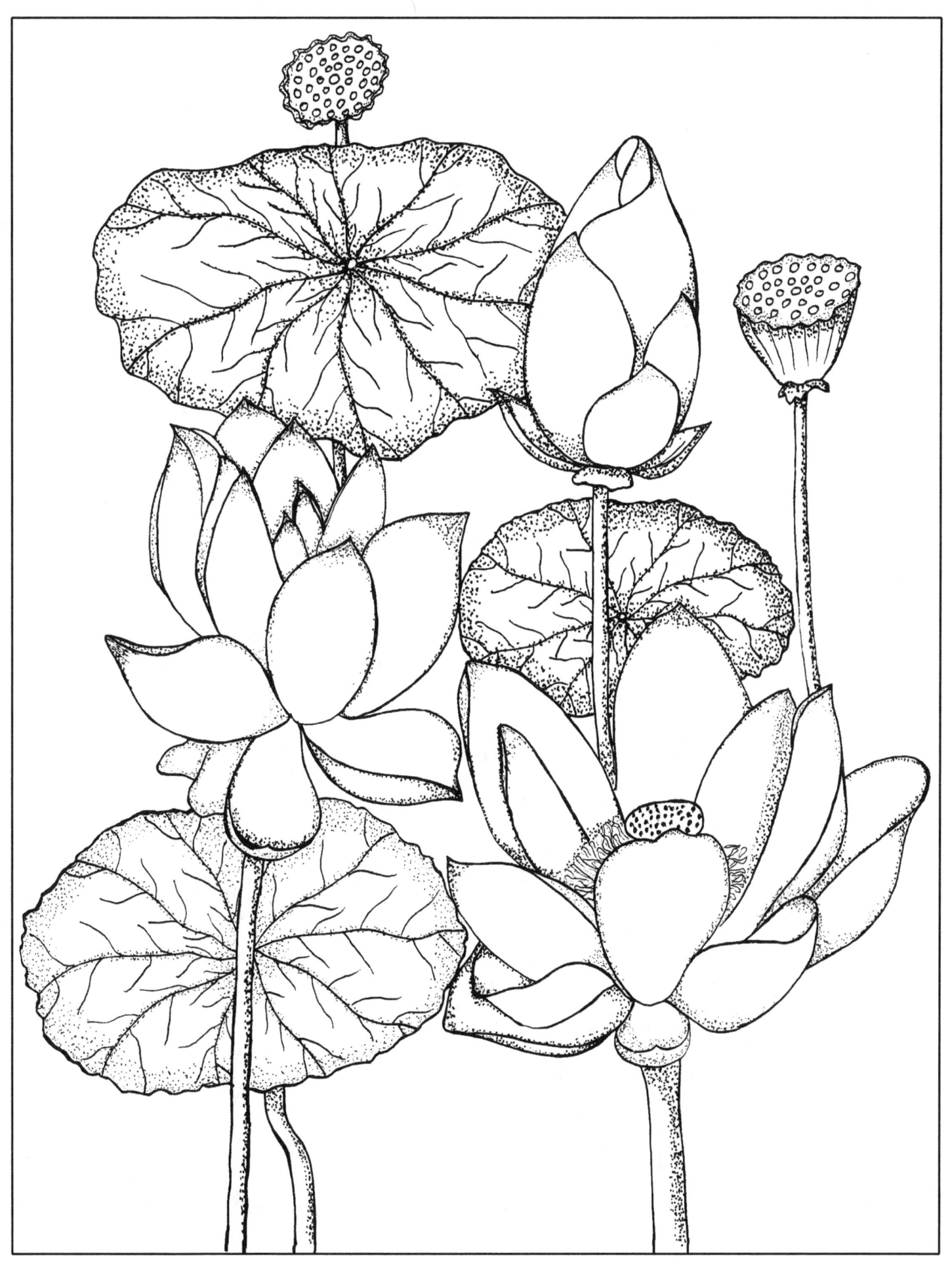

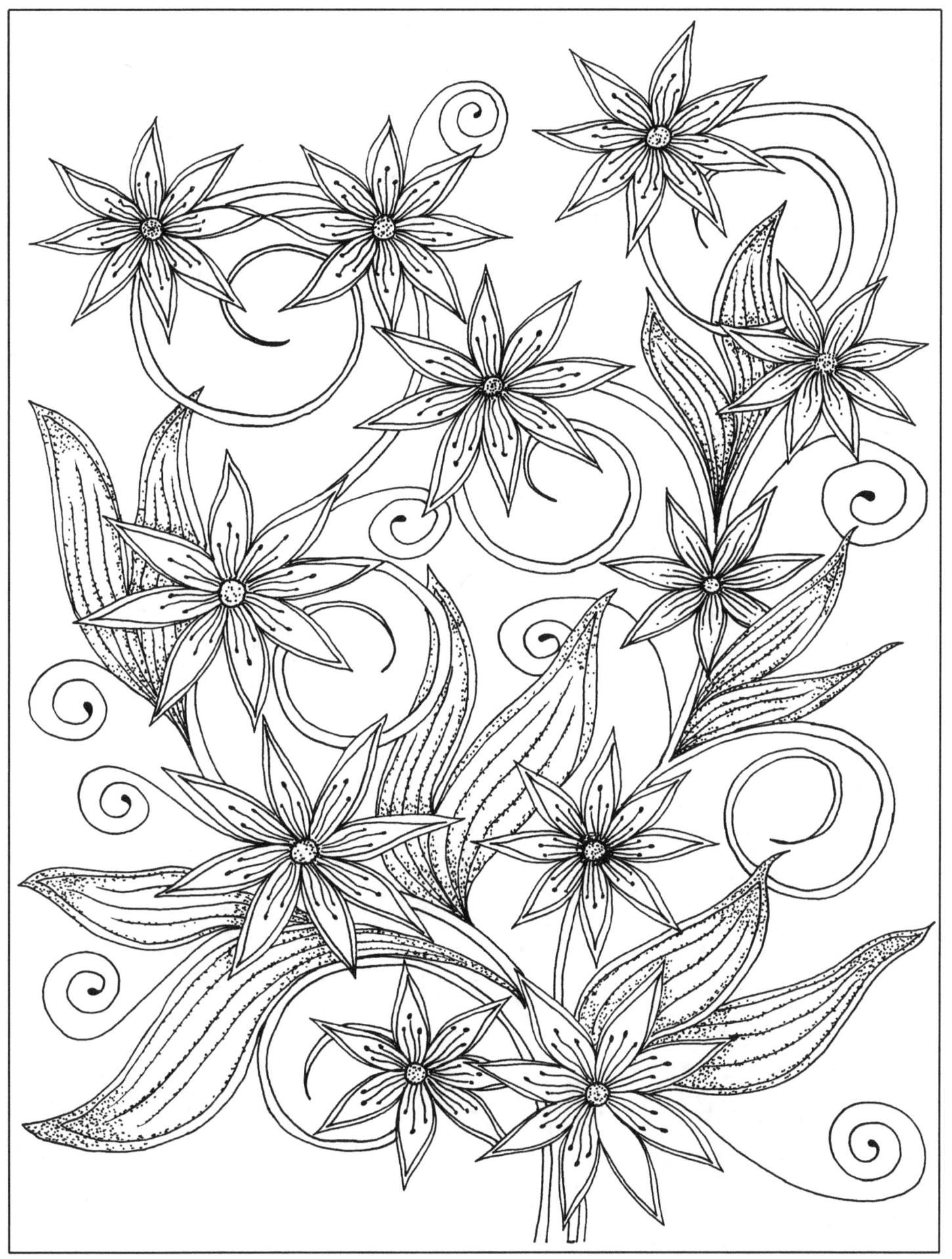

Contributing Artist
Neeti Goswami
Canada

www.artbyneeti.ca

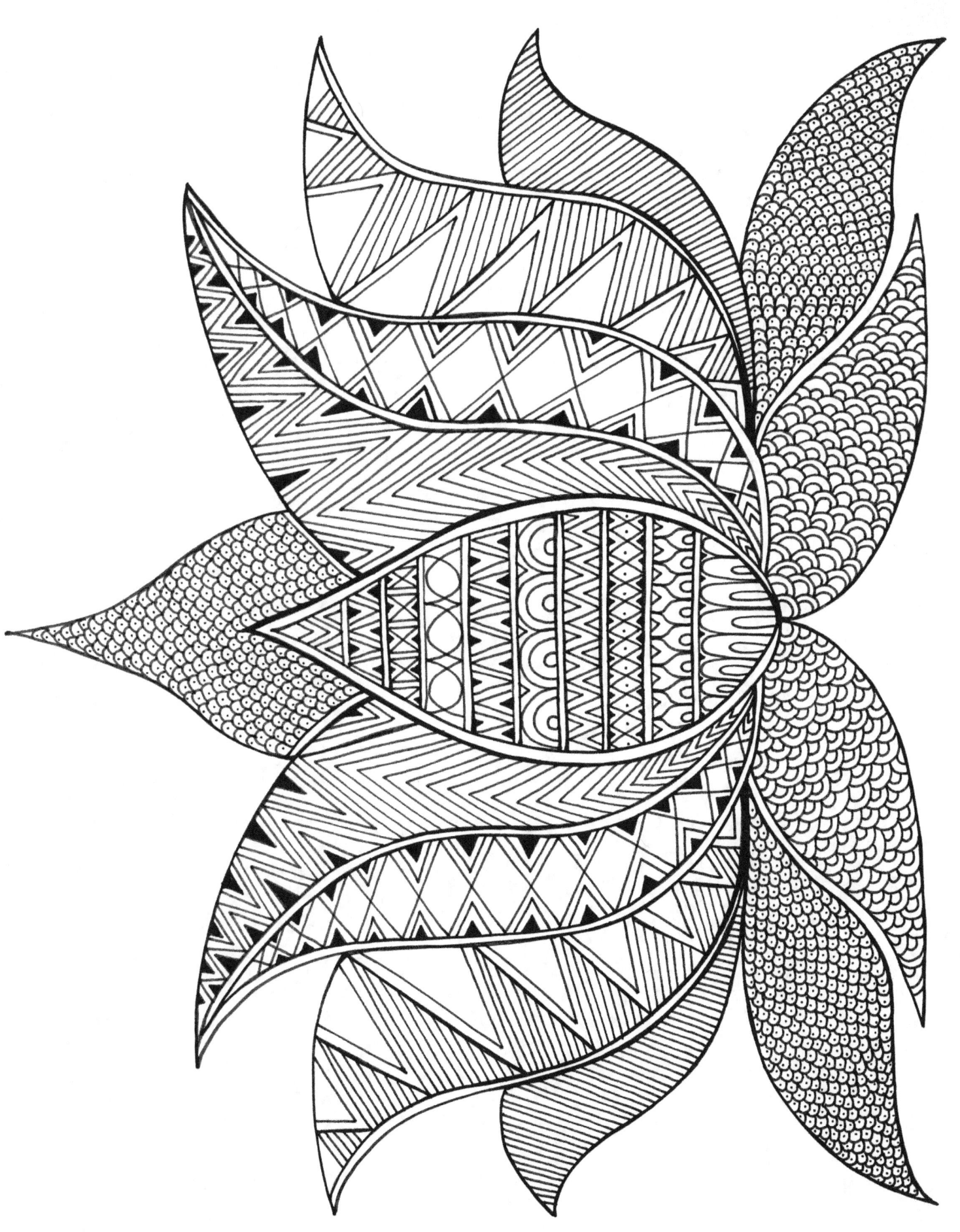

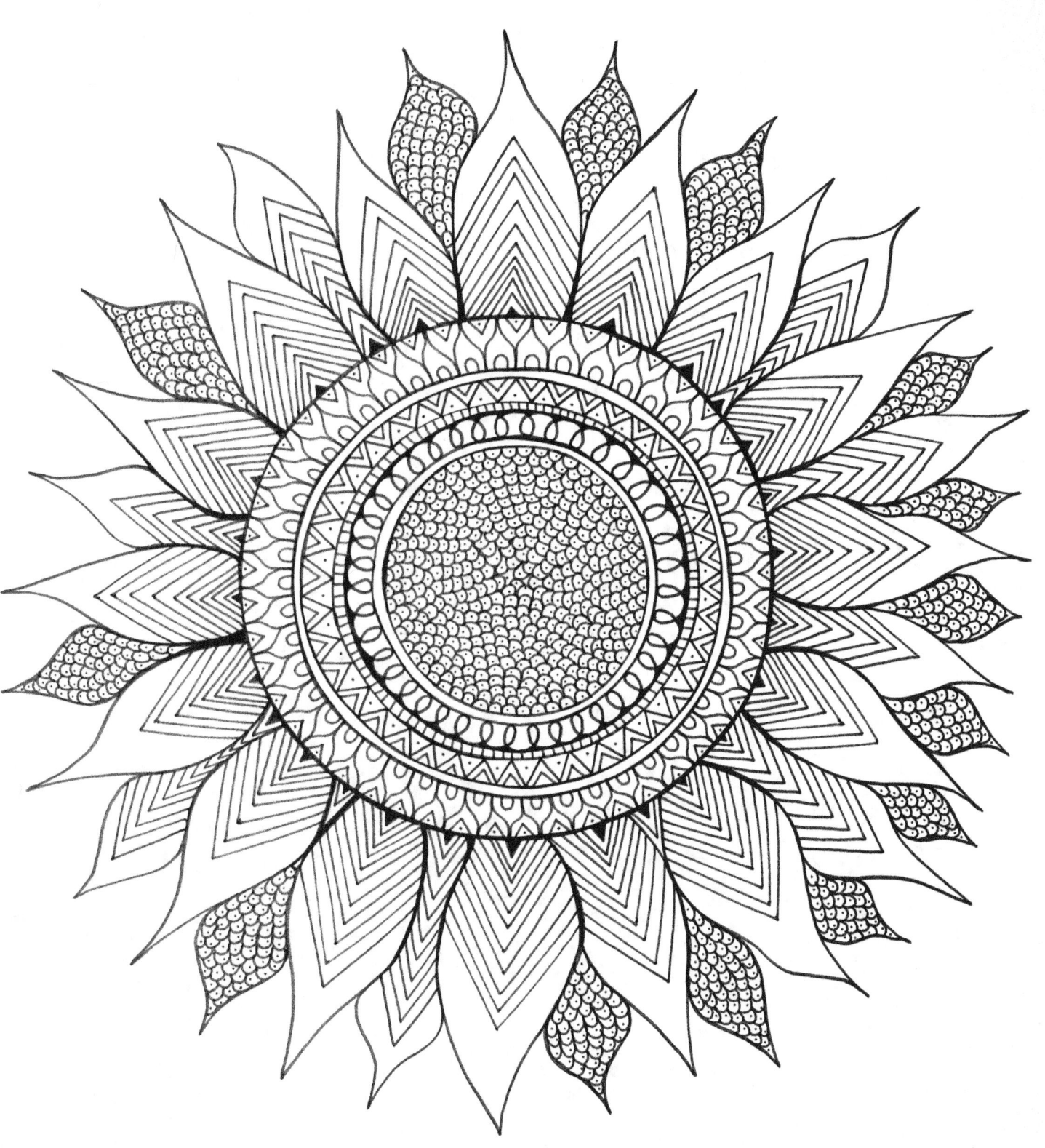

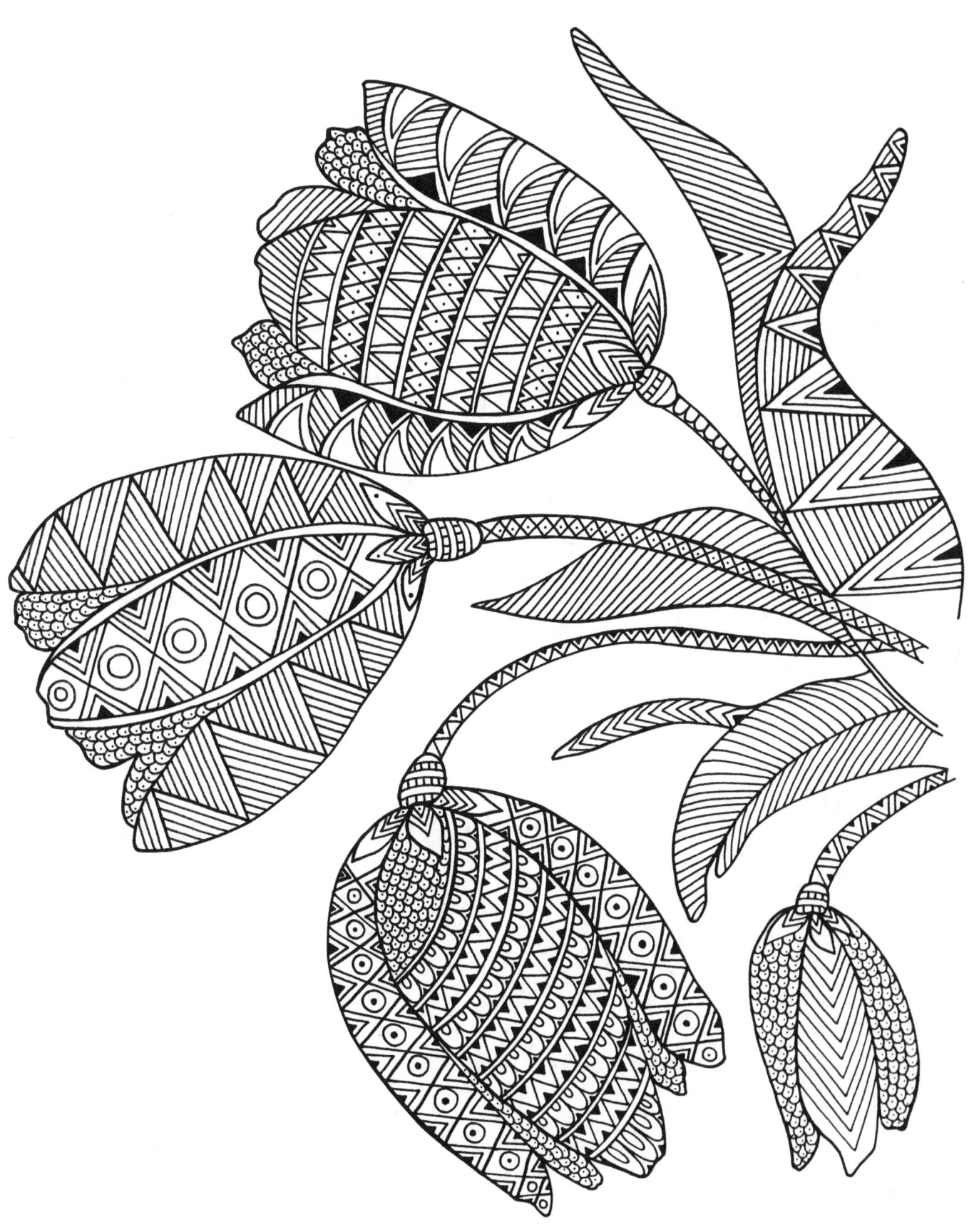

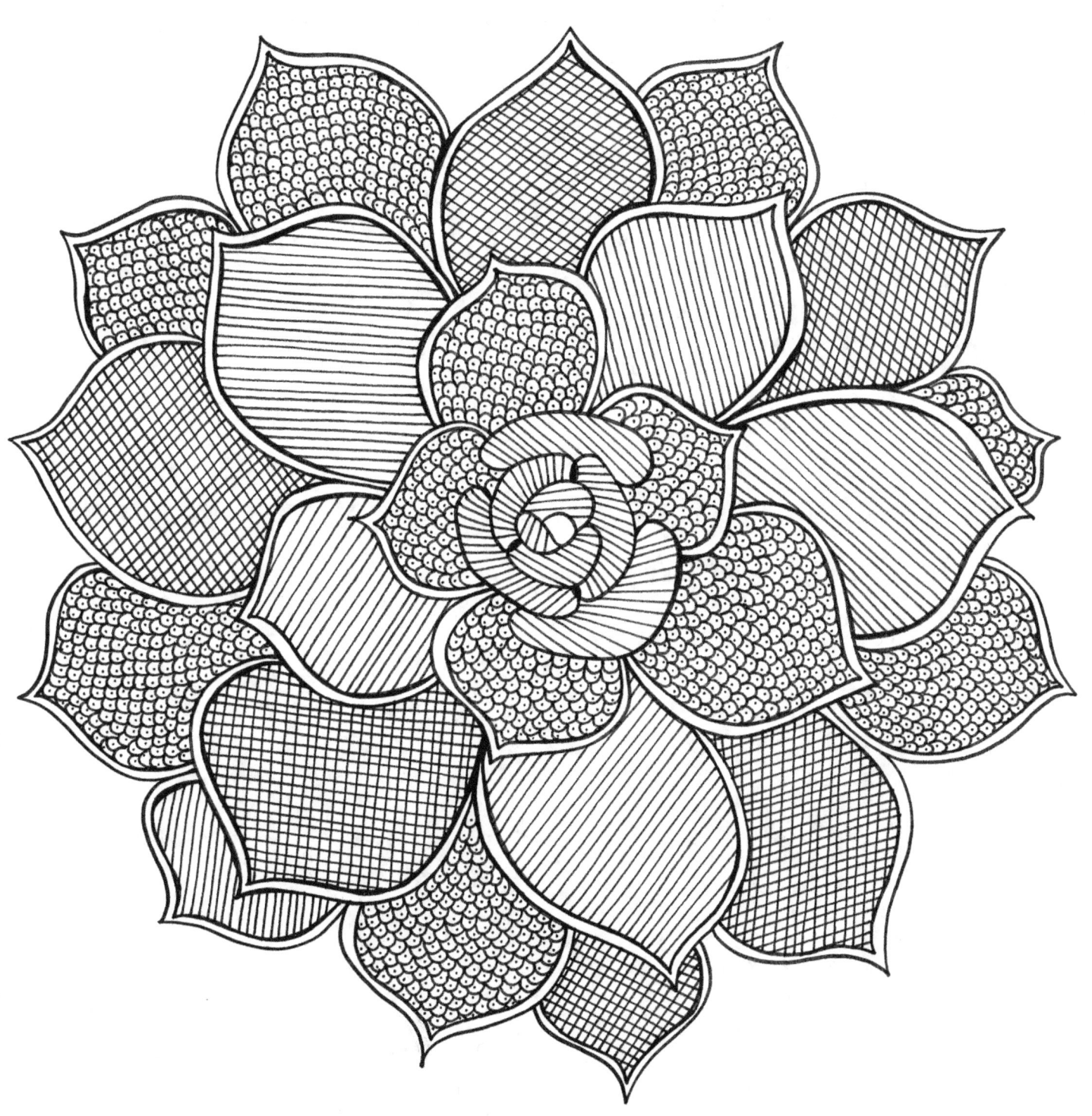

Contributing Artist
Yaya
France

Facebook : Les-gribouillis-de-yaya-georgia-merino

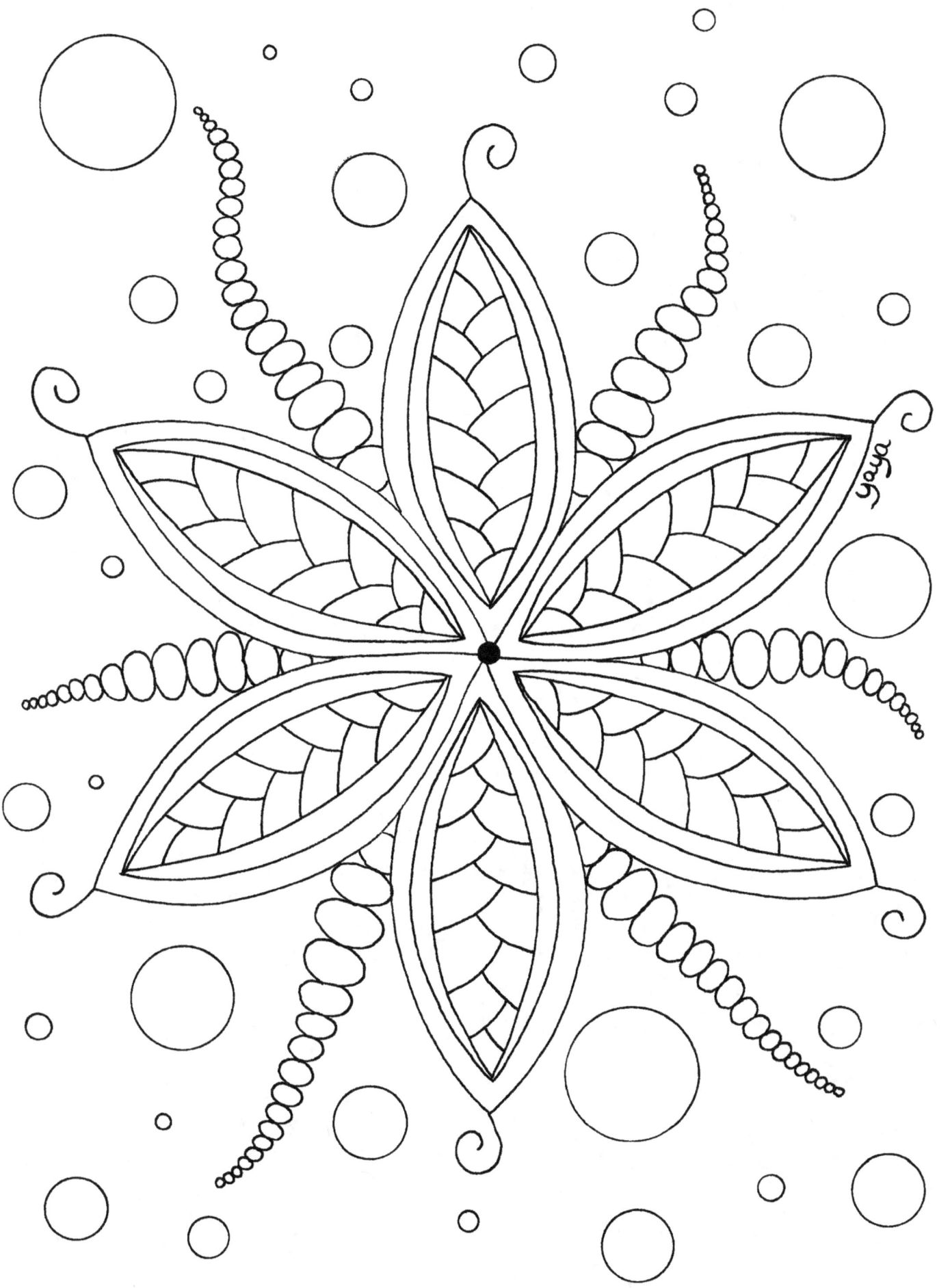

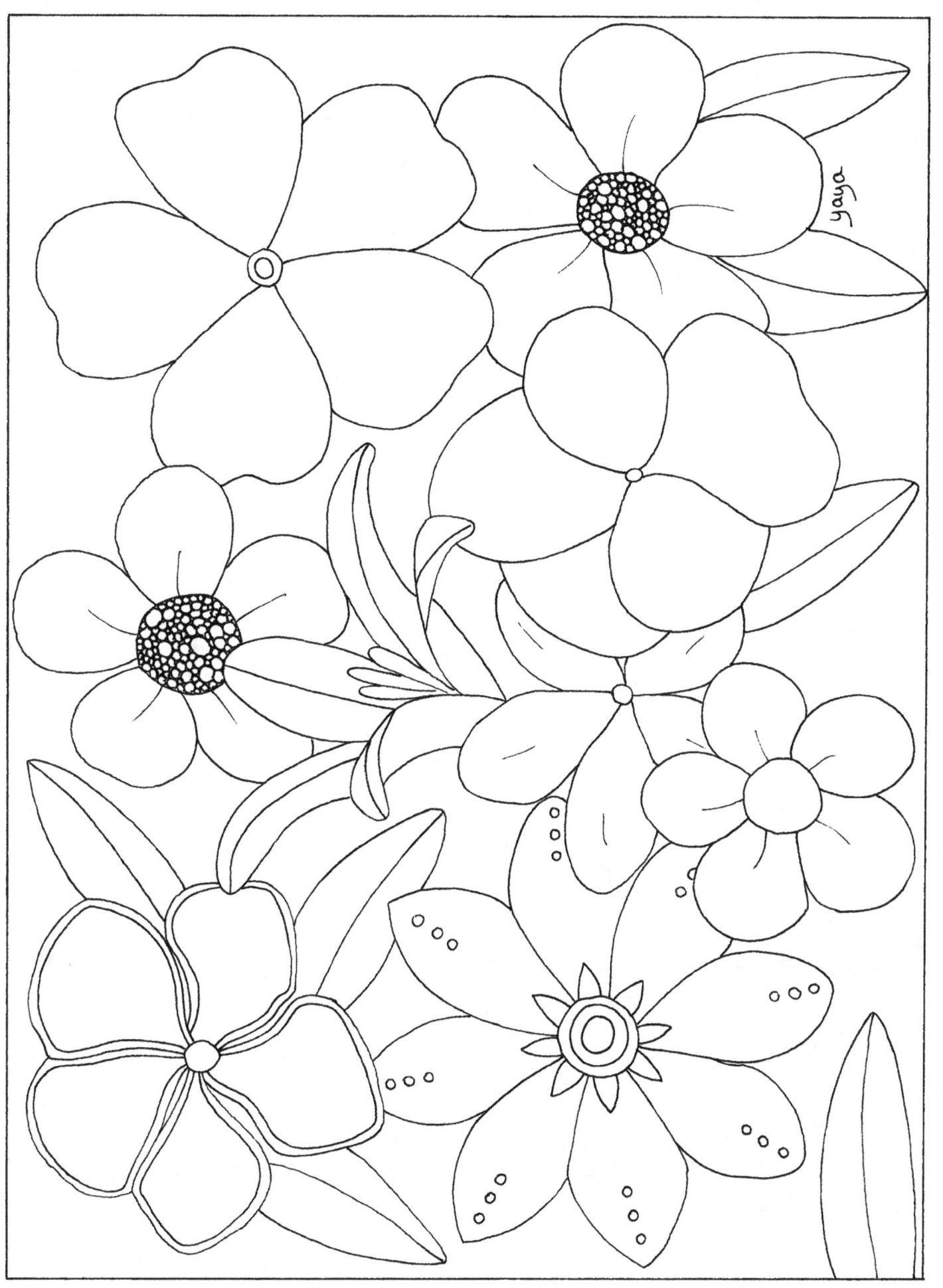

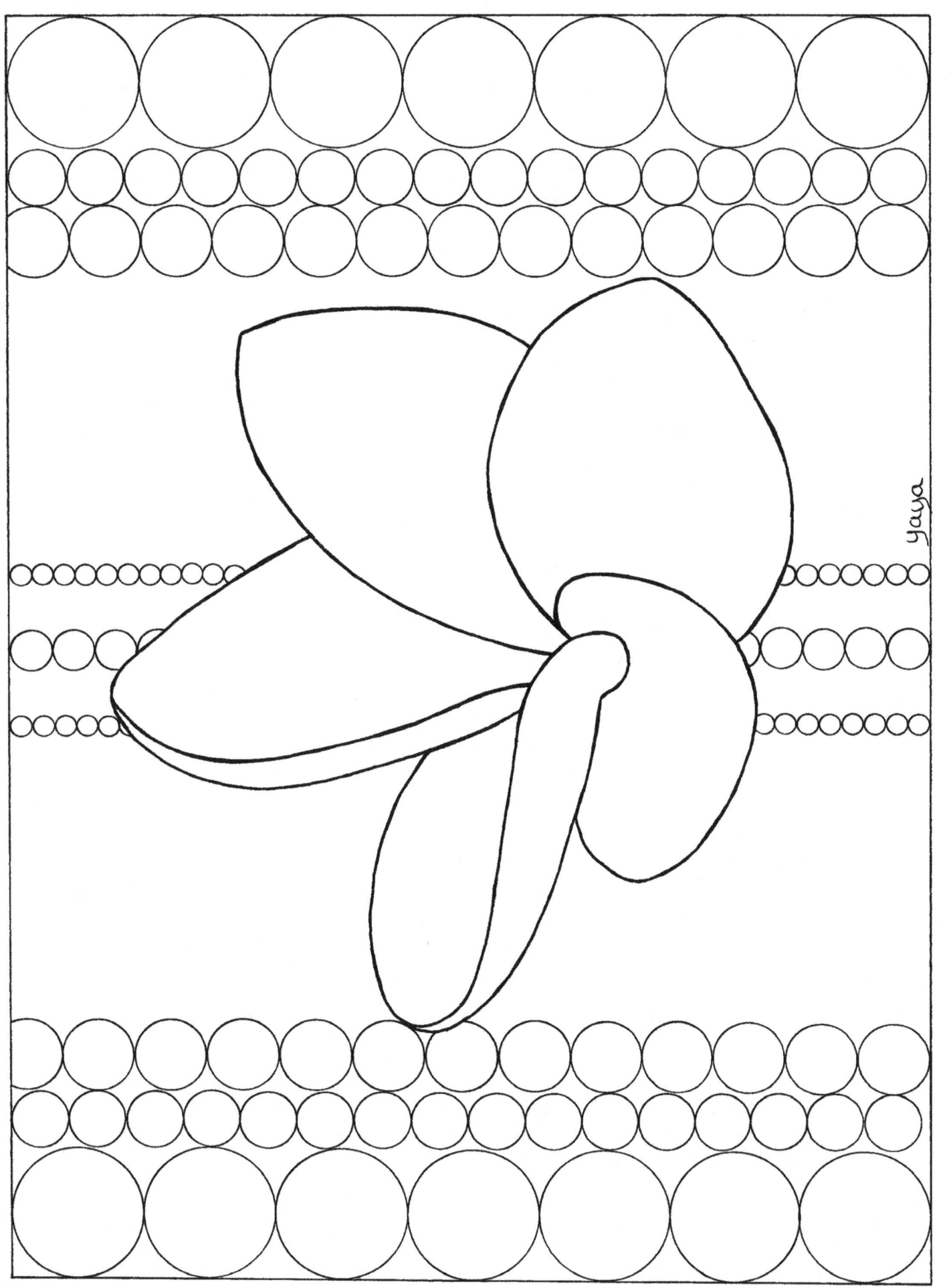

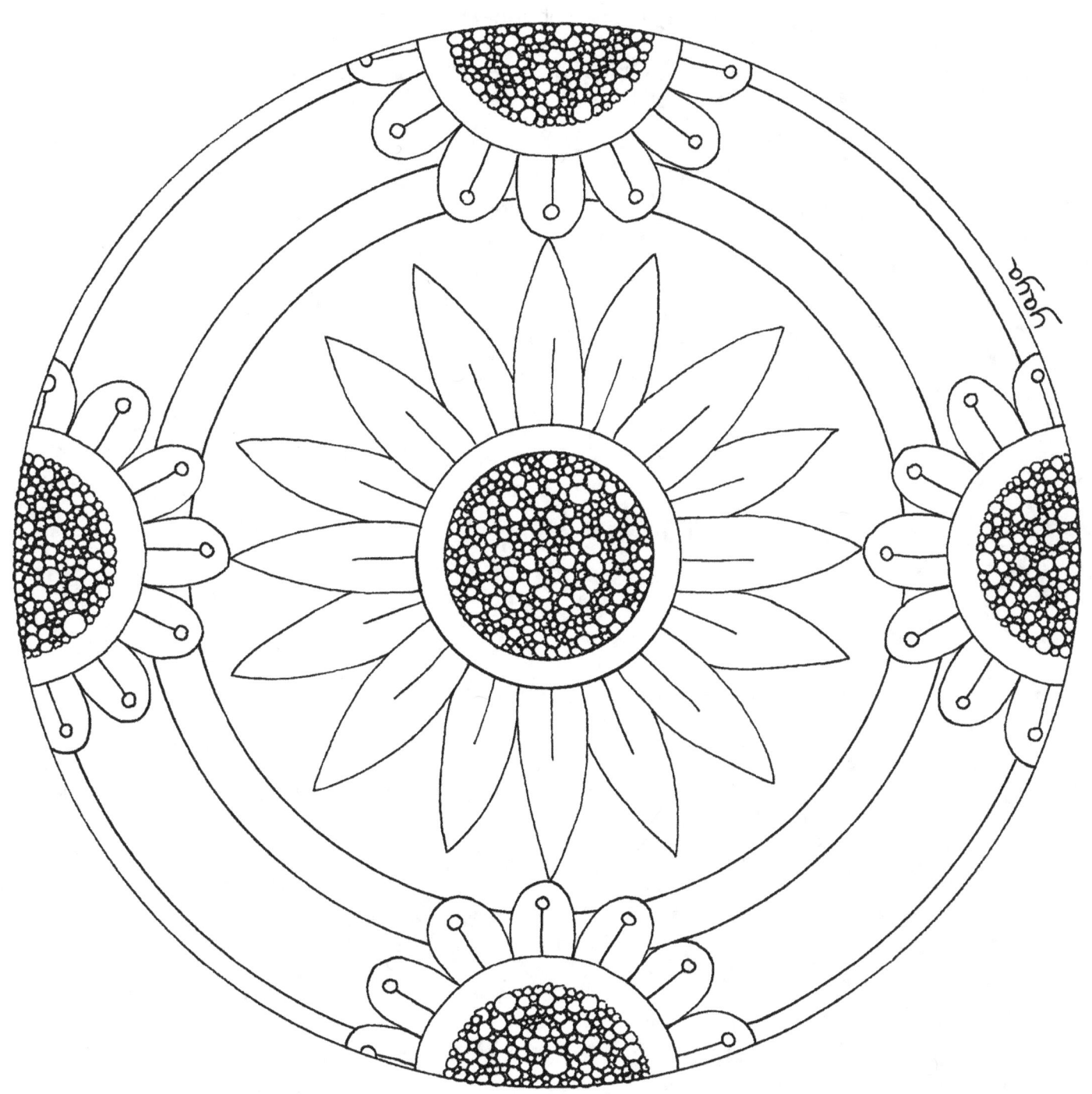

Contributing Artist
MWMS-Johanna Ans
The Netherlands

Blog : mywaymystylejohannaans.wordpress.com

Facebook : Johanna-Ans-My-creative-site

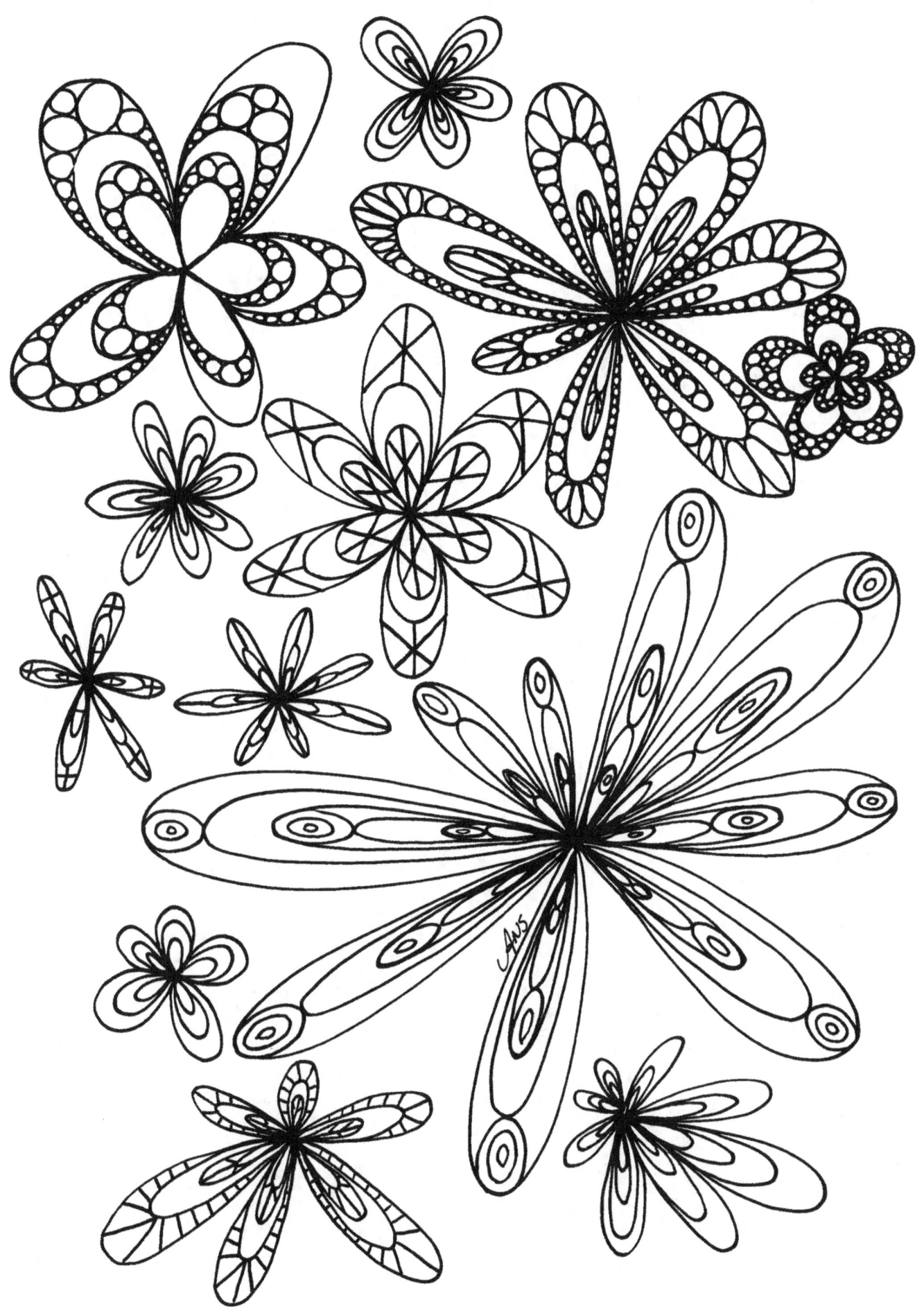

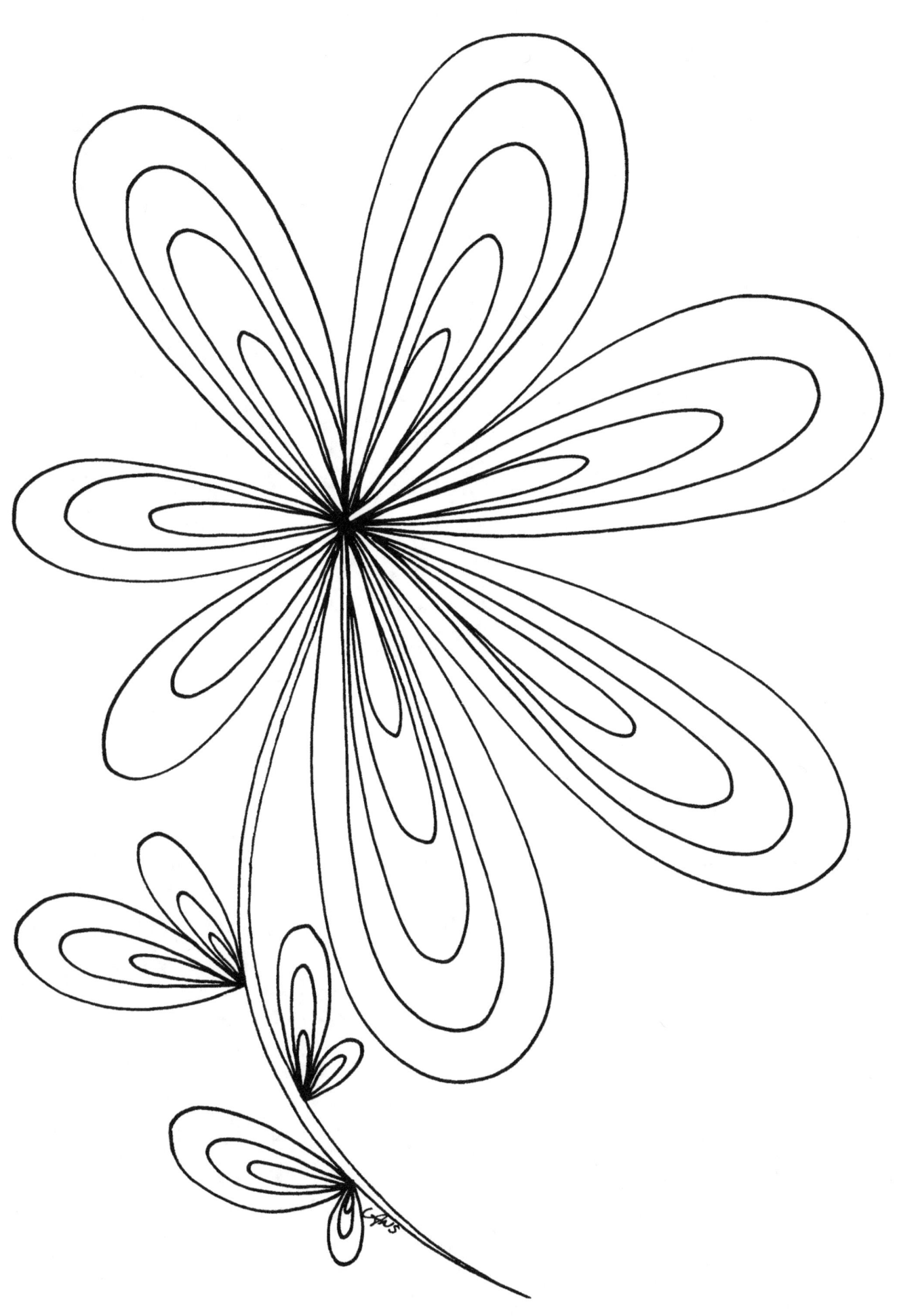

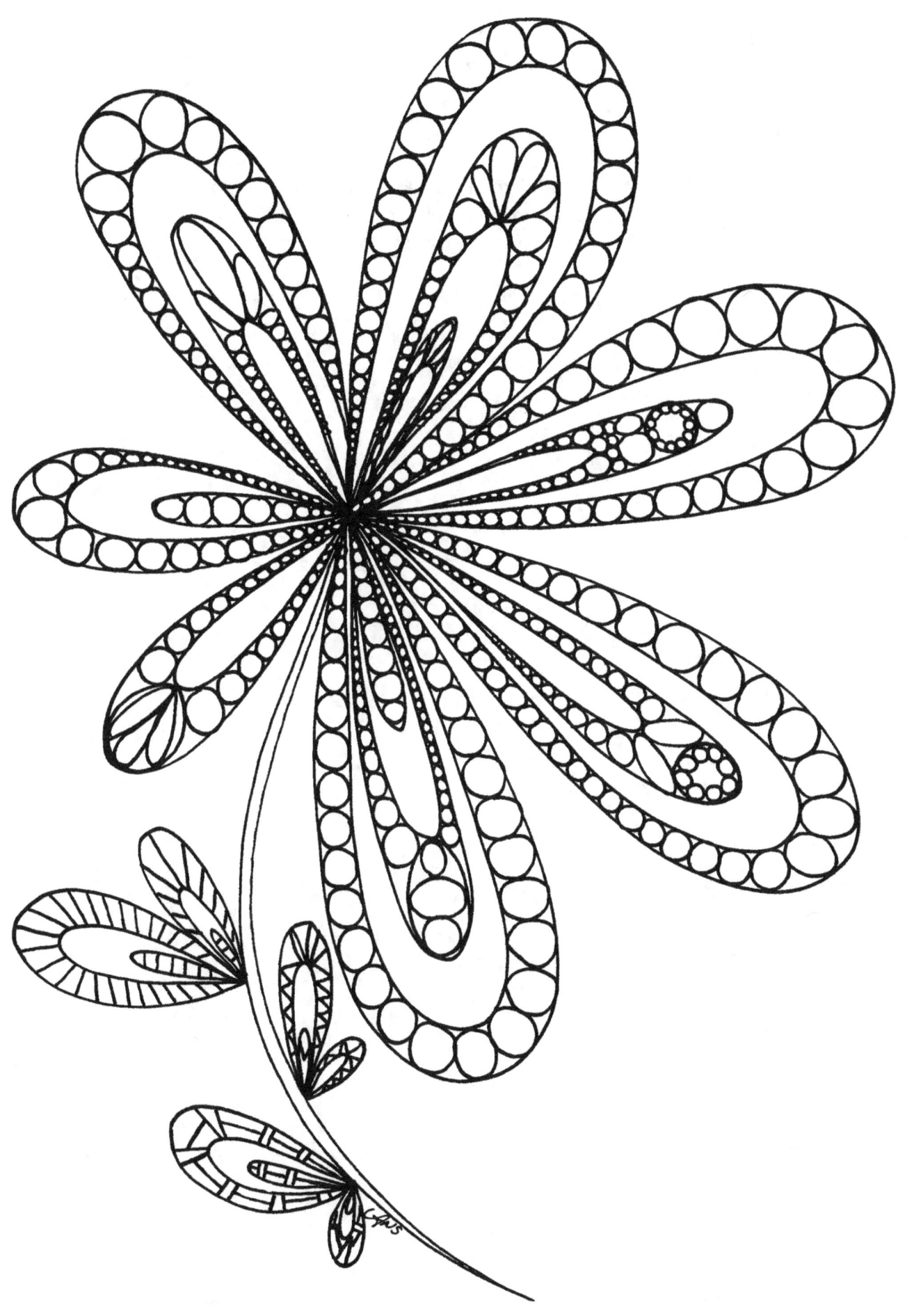

Contributing Artist
Ellen Wolters
The Netherlands

http://www.tekenpraktijkdeinnerlijkewereld.blogspot.nl/
http://ellenstraties.blogspot.nl/
https://www.youtube.com/user/DIWEllenWolters

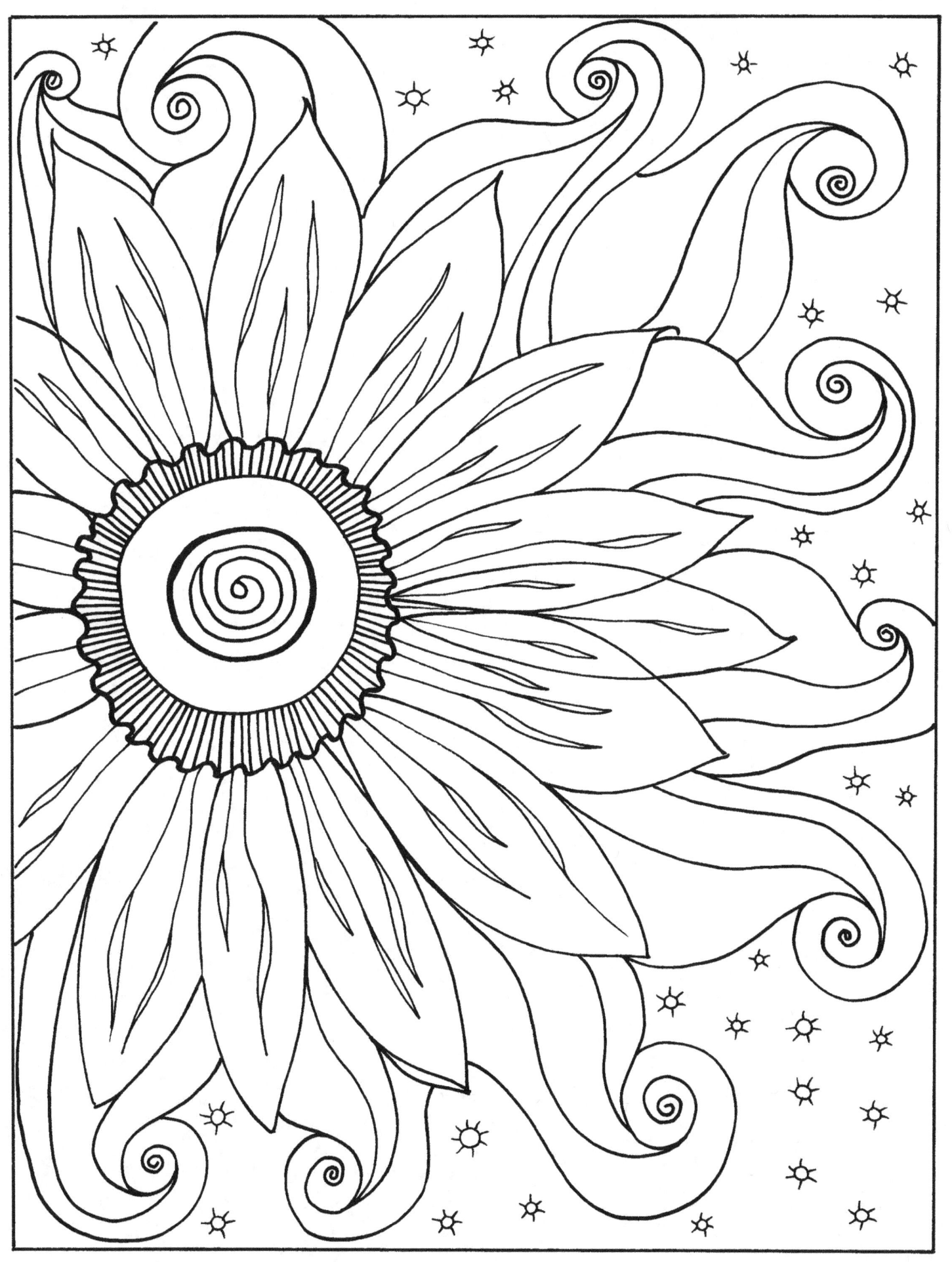

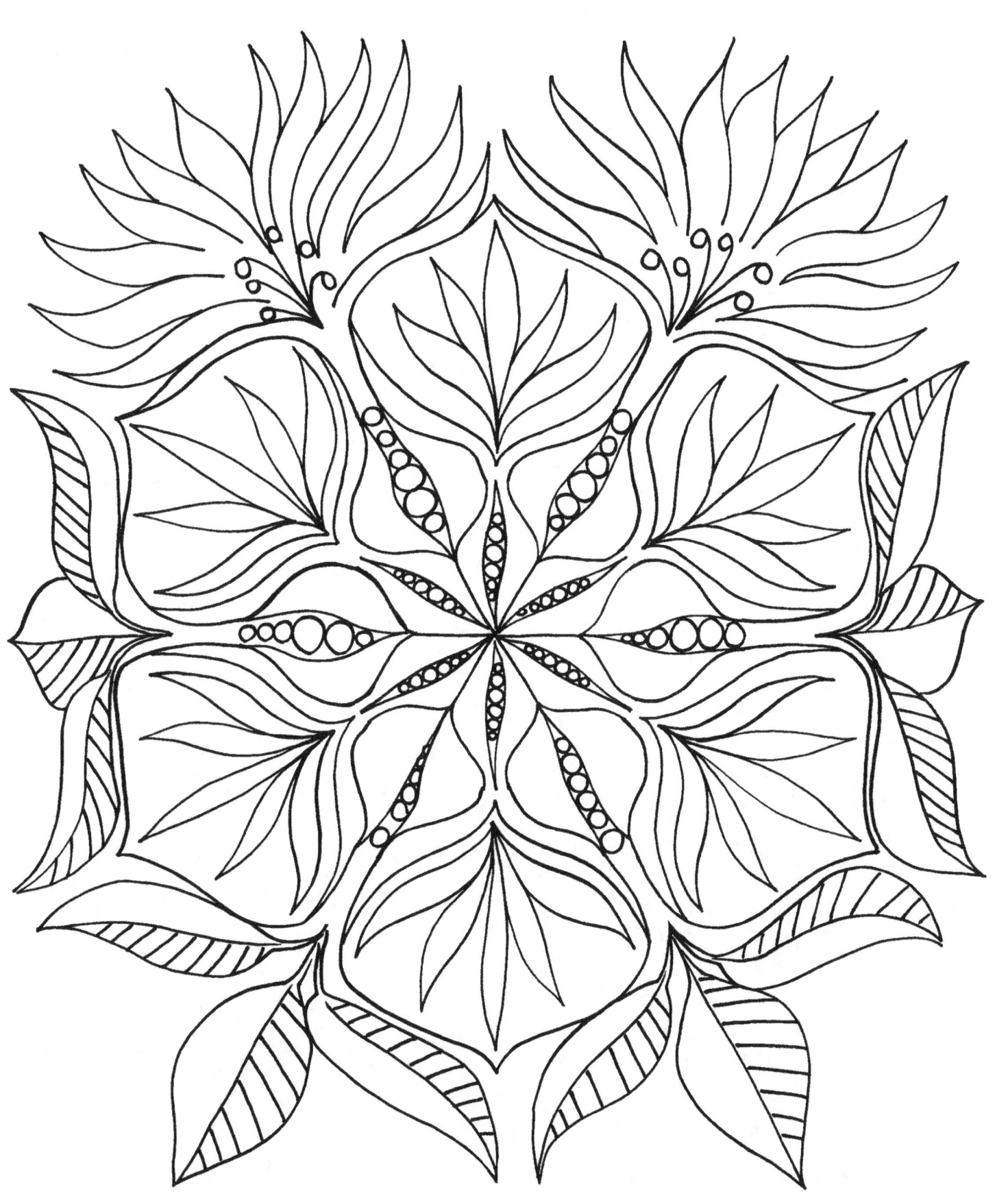

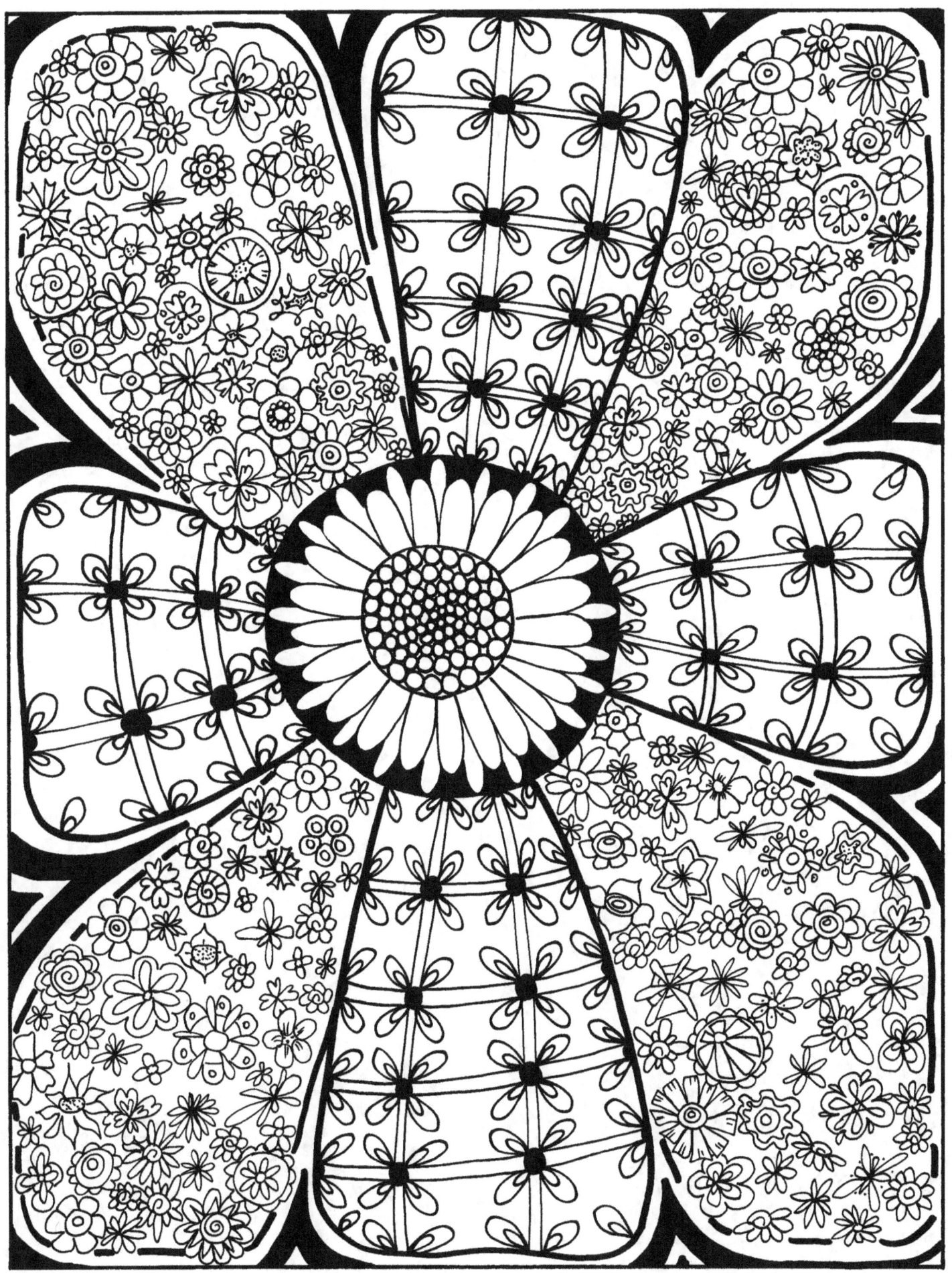

Contributing Artist
Adriana Graciela Volpe
Argentina

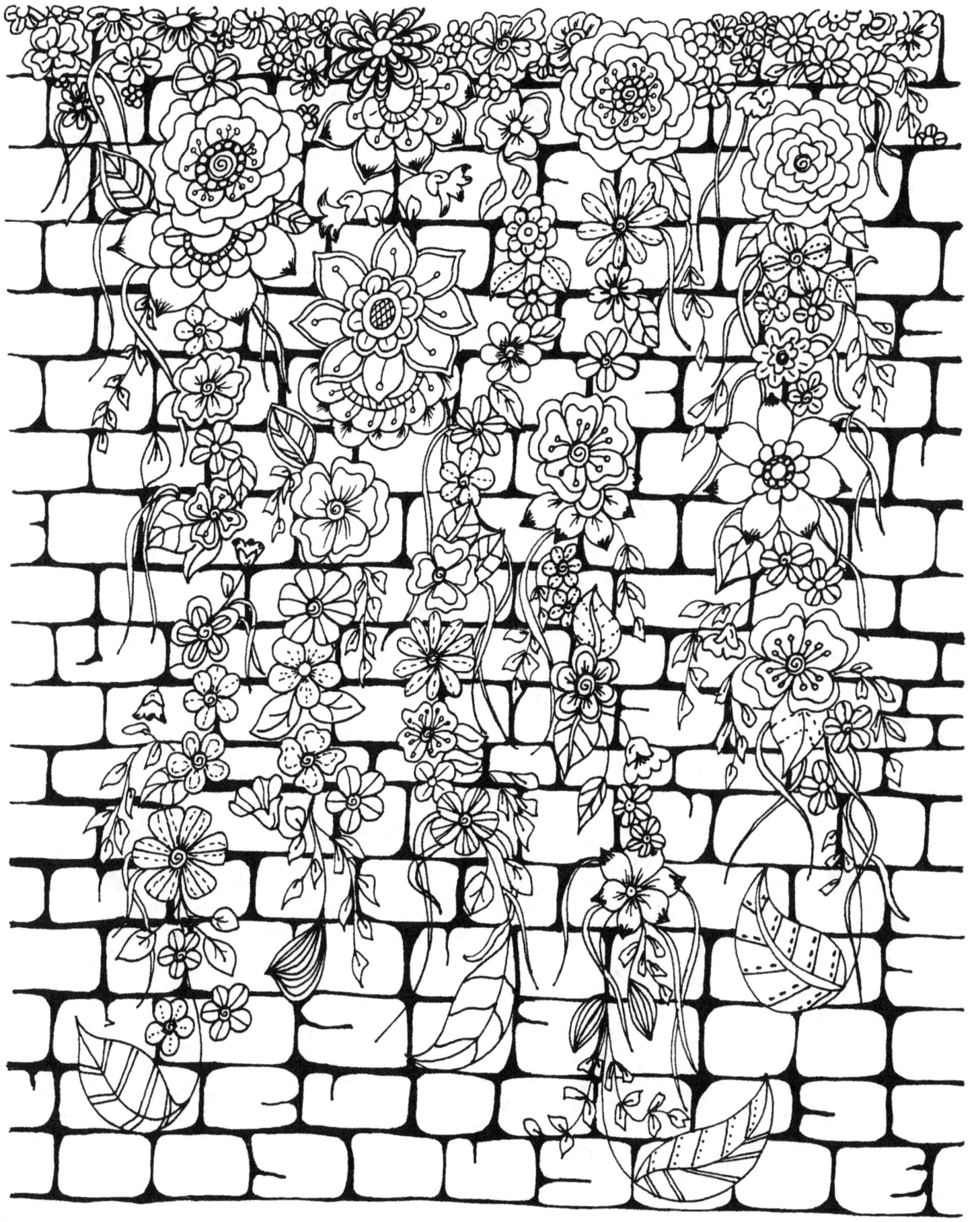

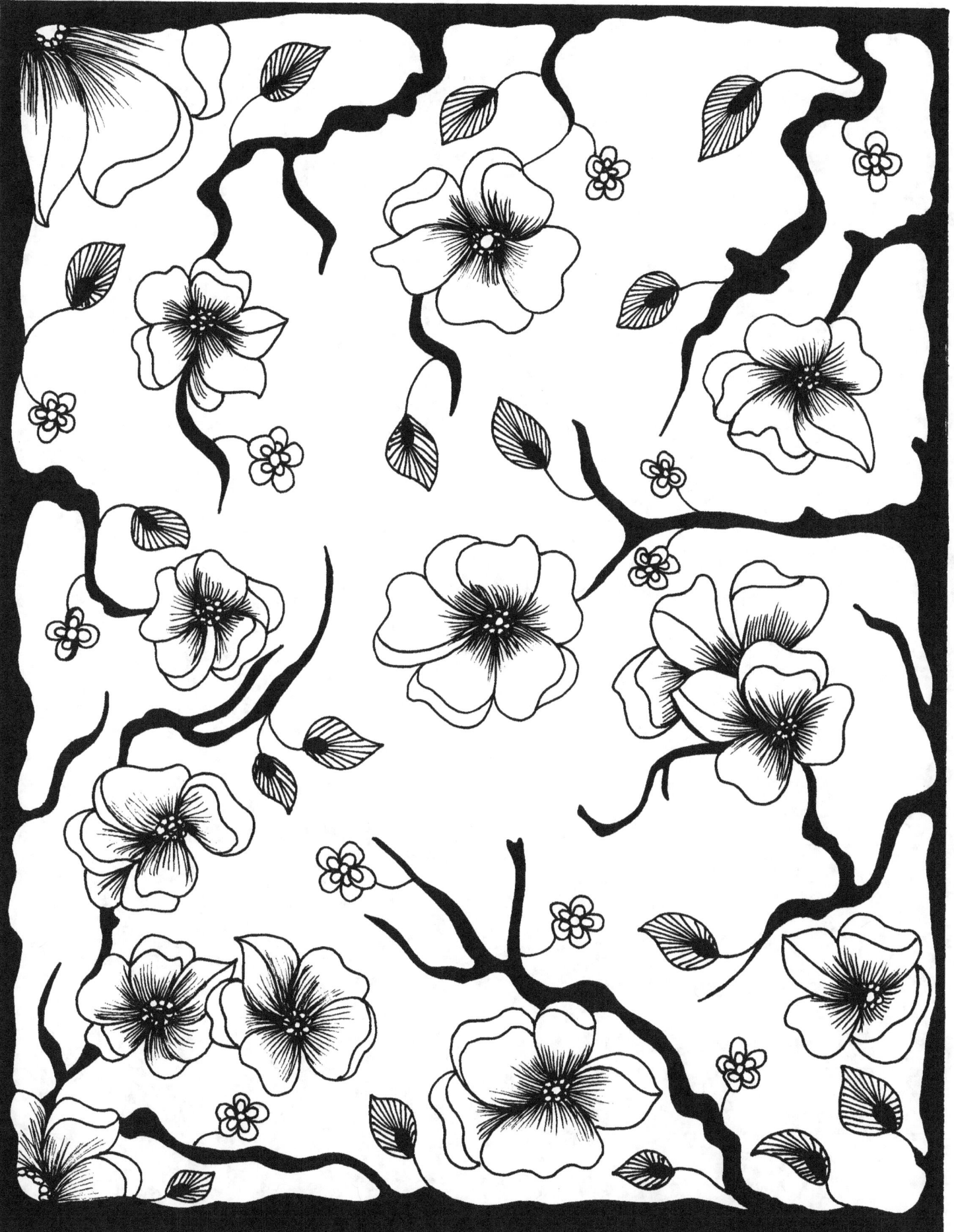

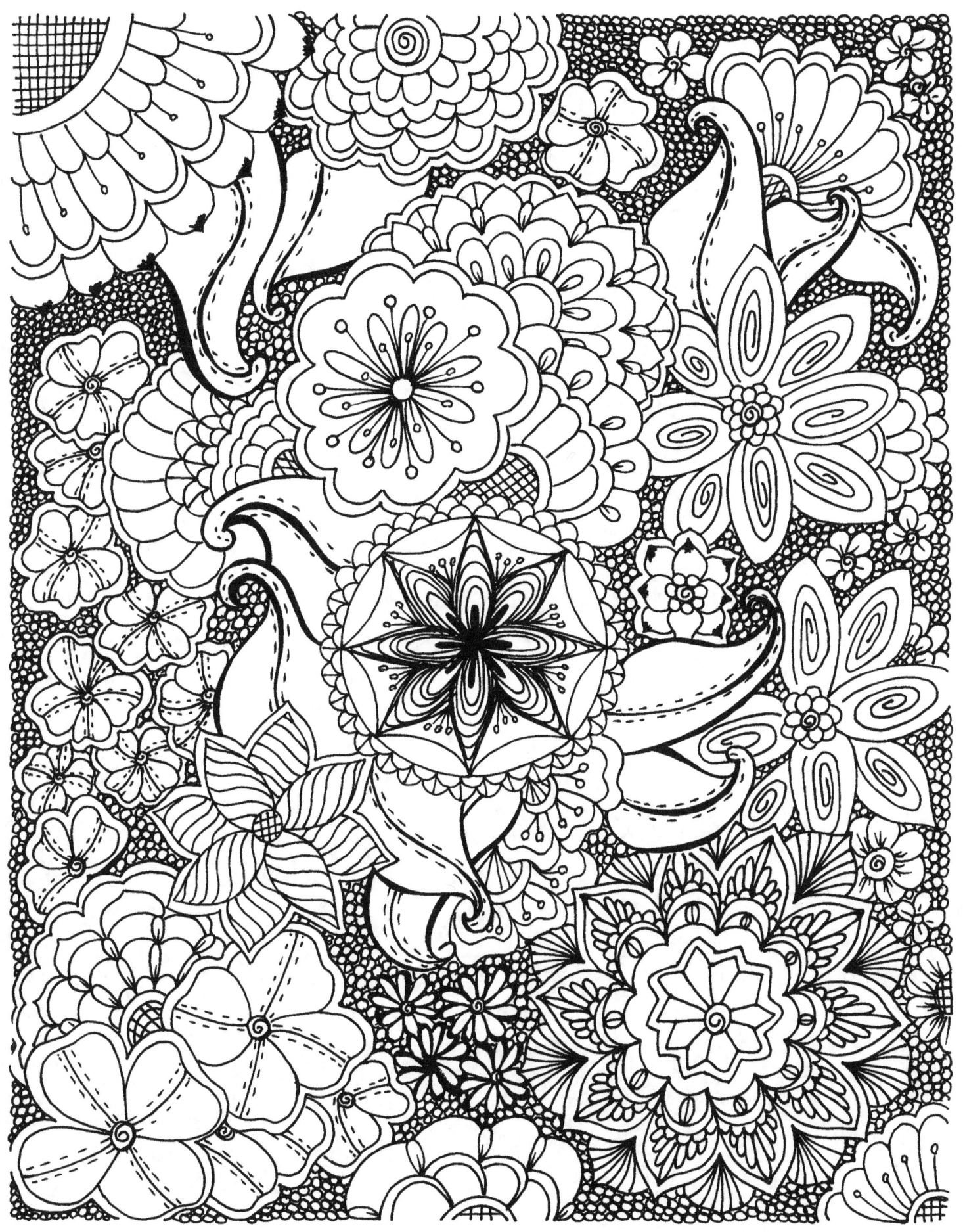

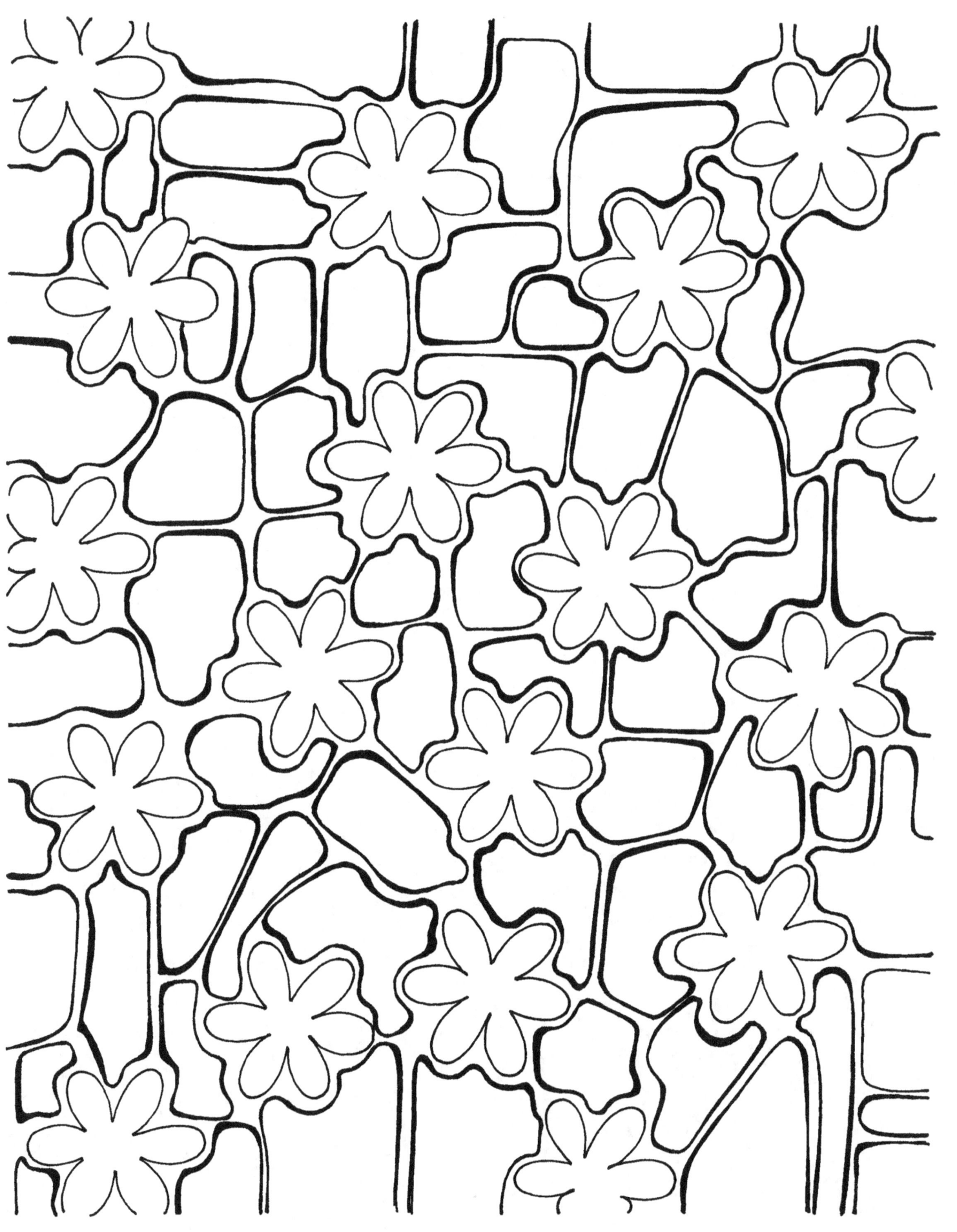

Contributing Artist
Alfred E. Villanueva
Philippines
Facebook : viworksart2015

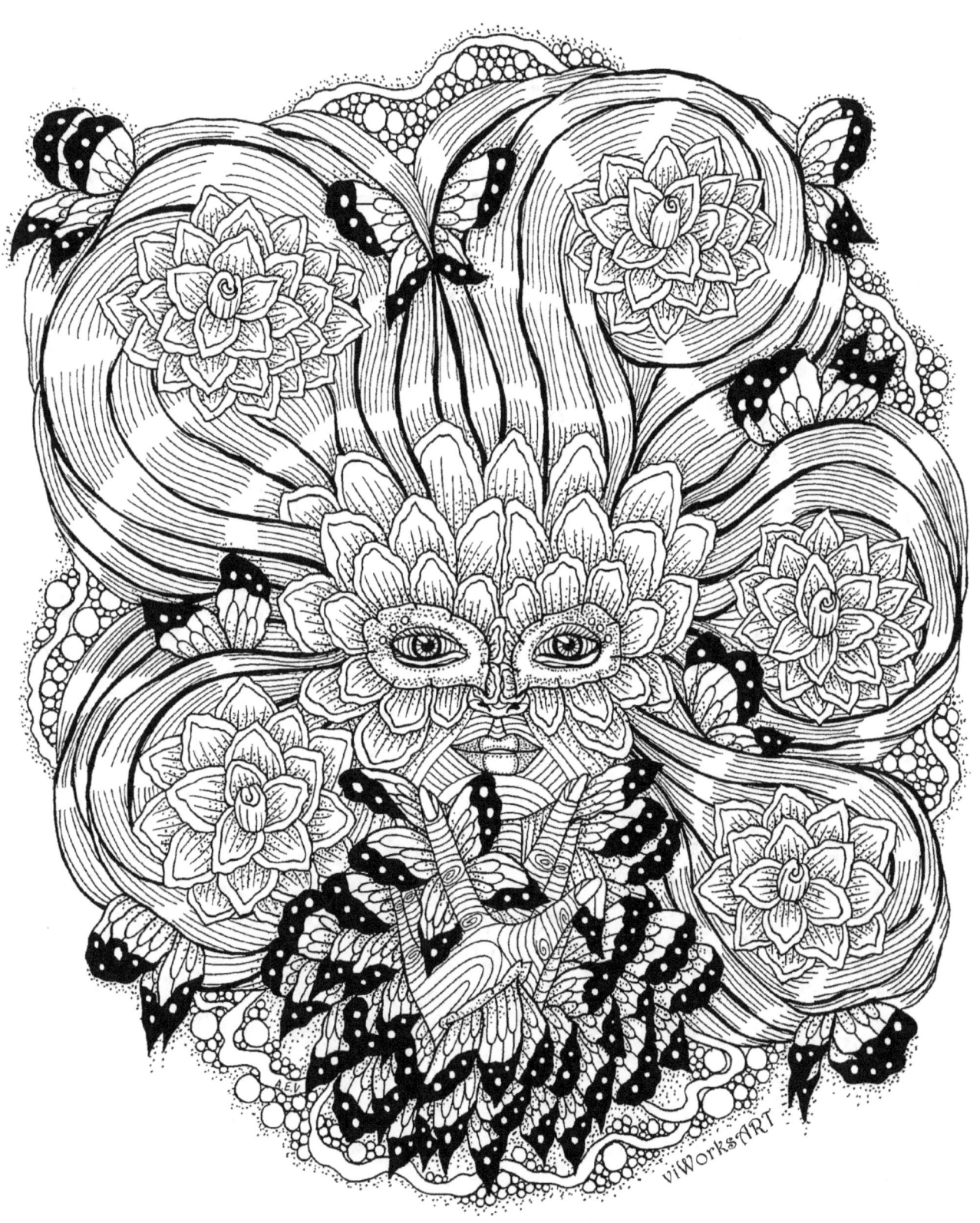

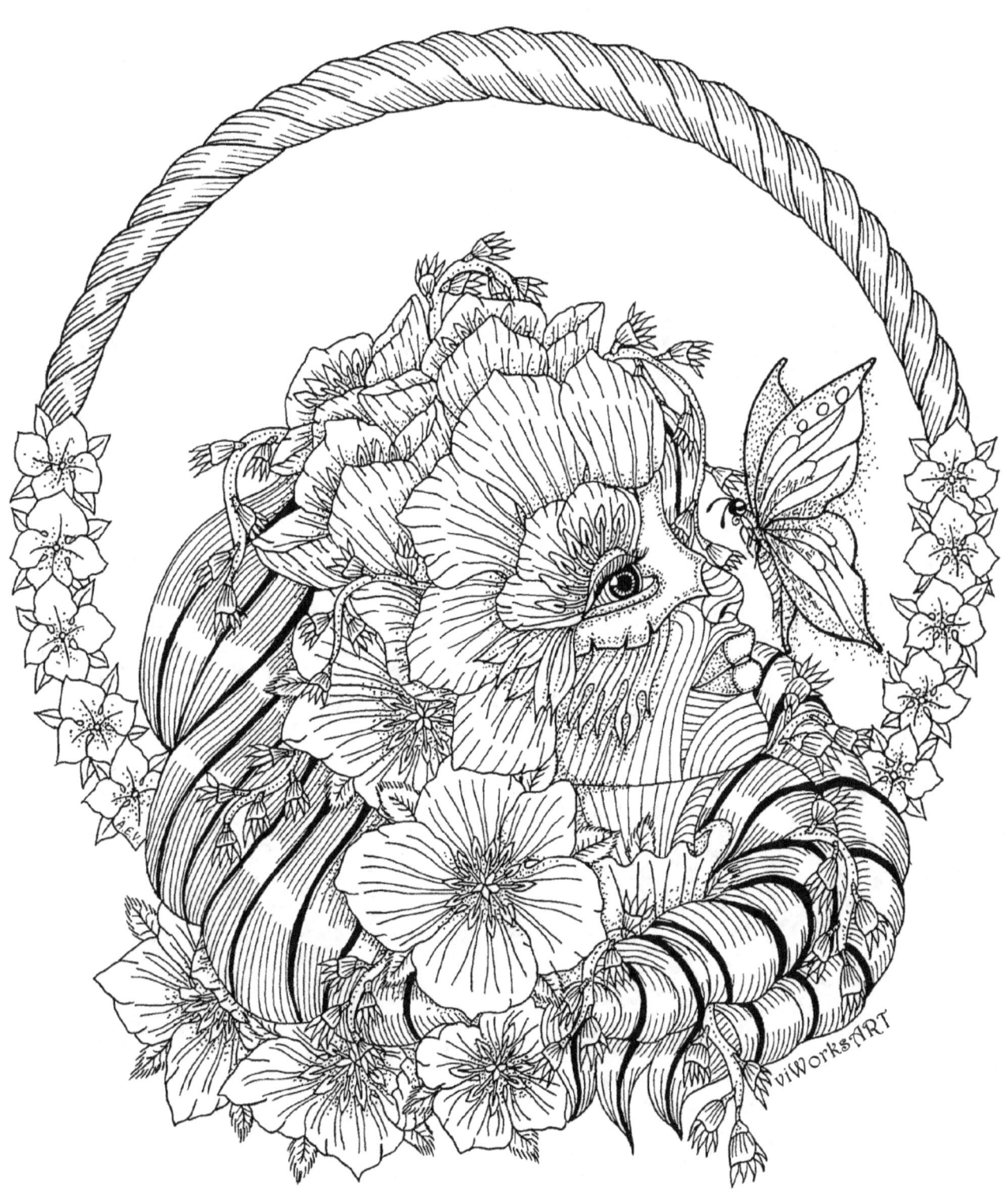

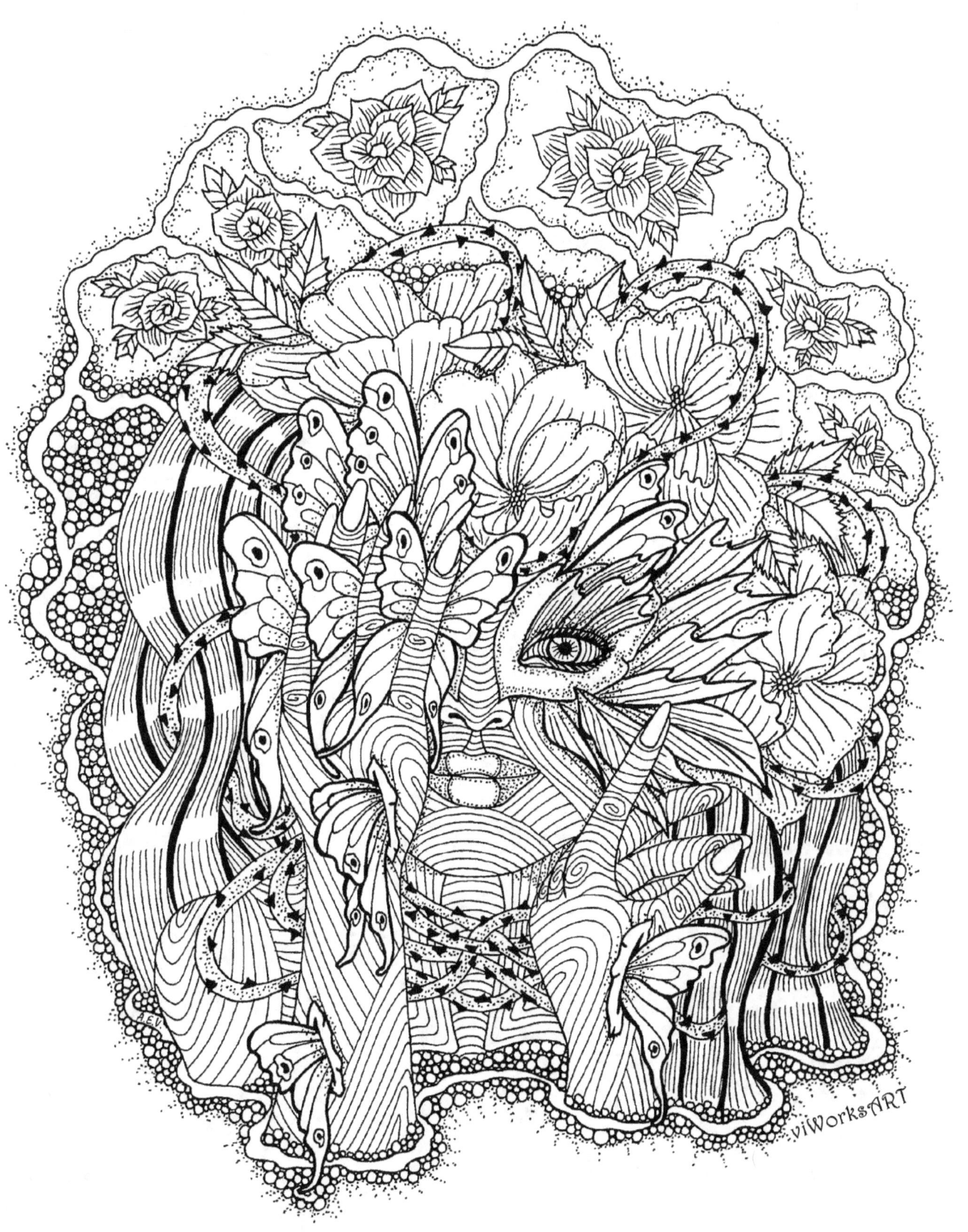

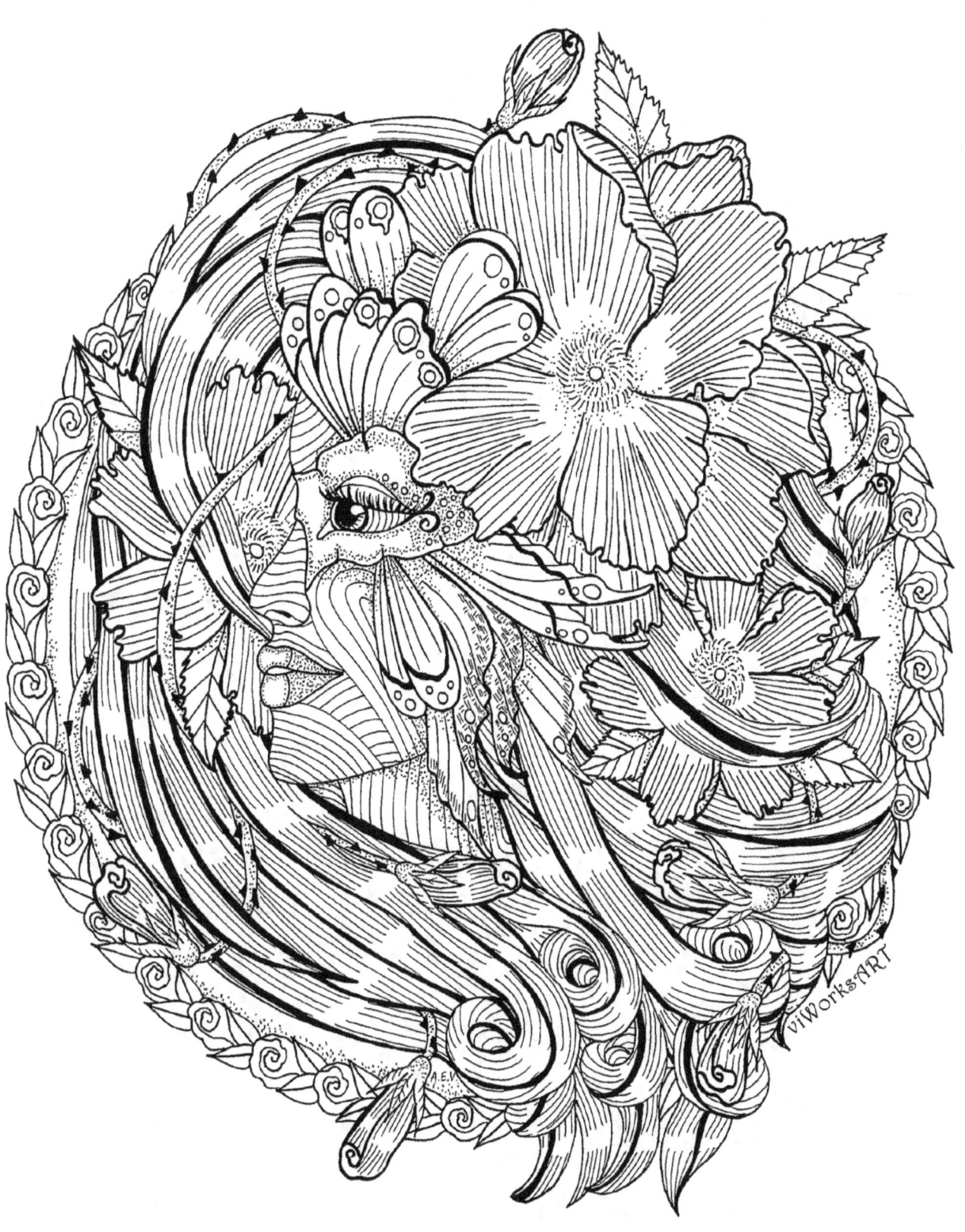

Contributing Artist
Maud Feral Chauveau
(MFC)
France

« MFC - Peinture, graphisme & illustration »

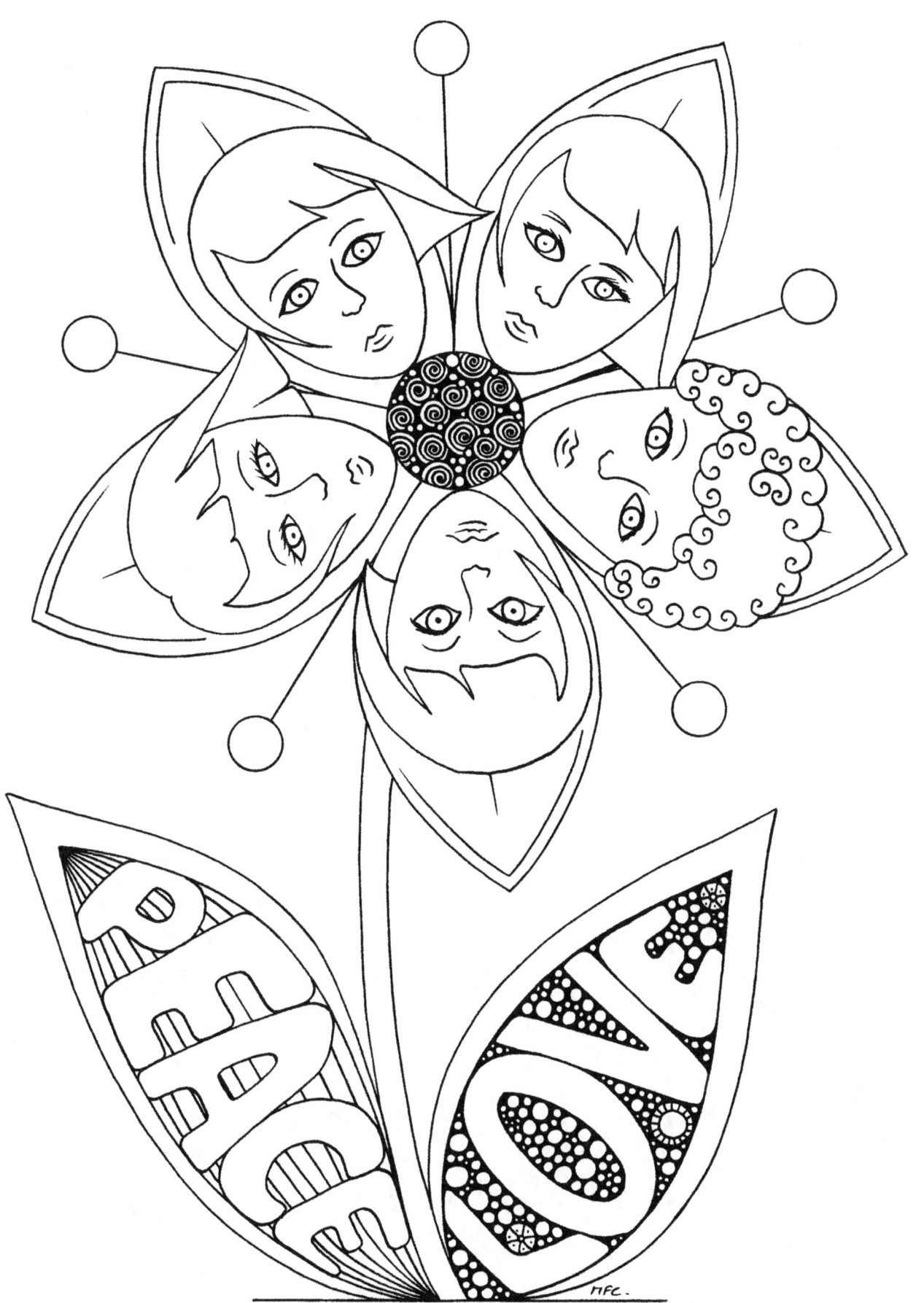

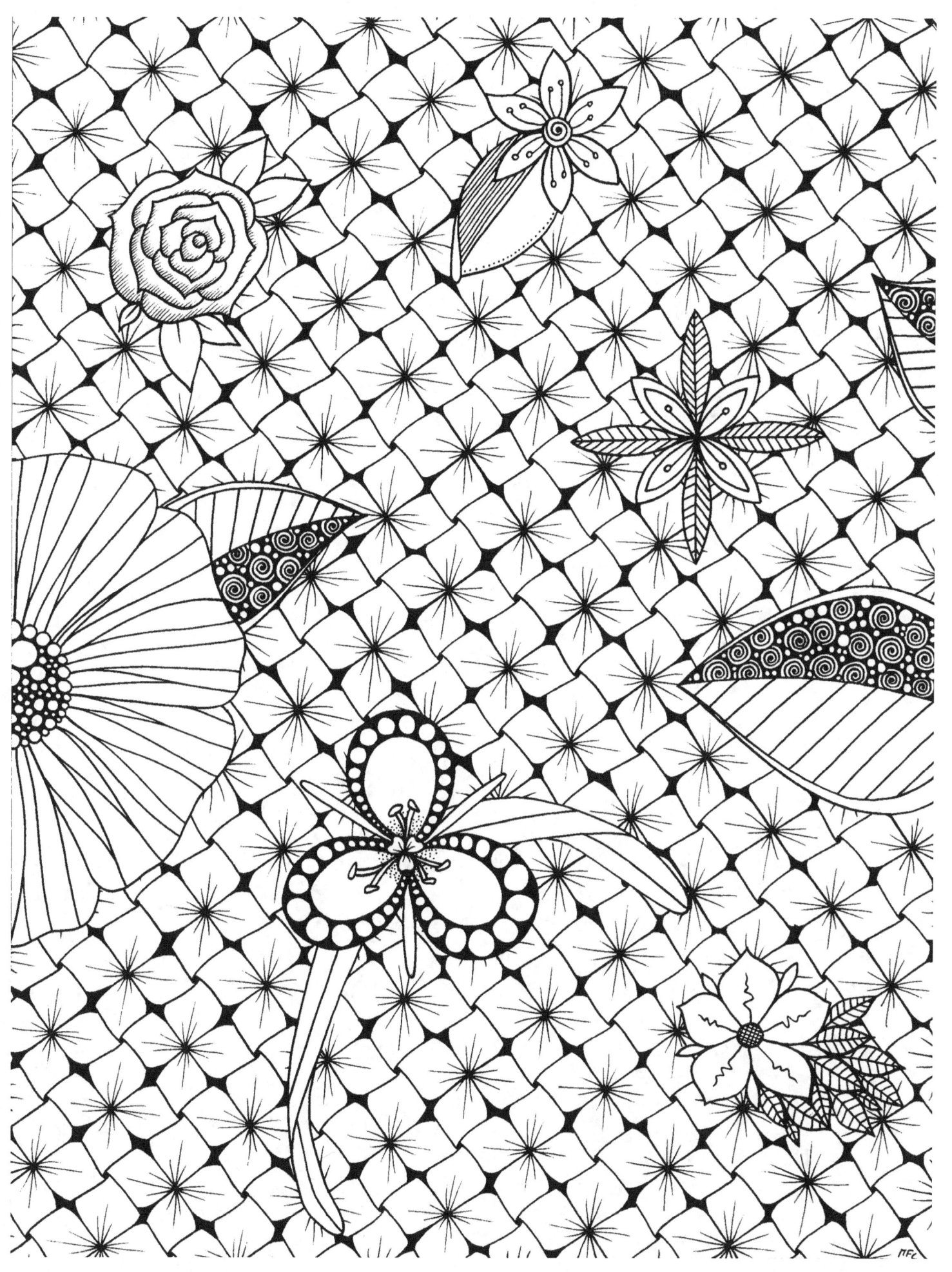

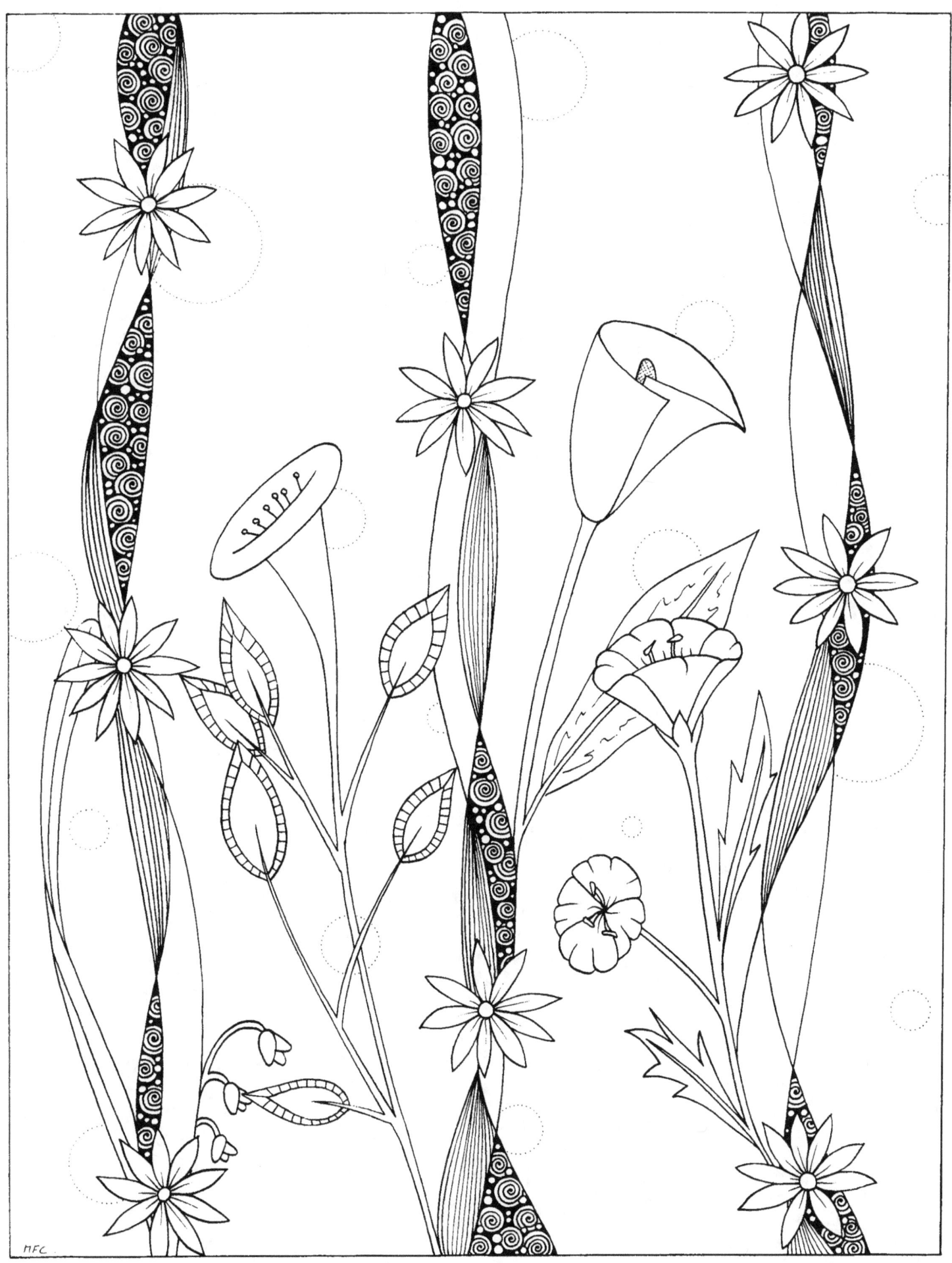

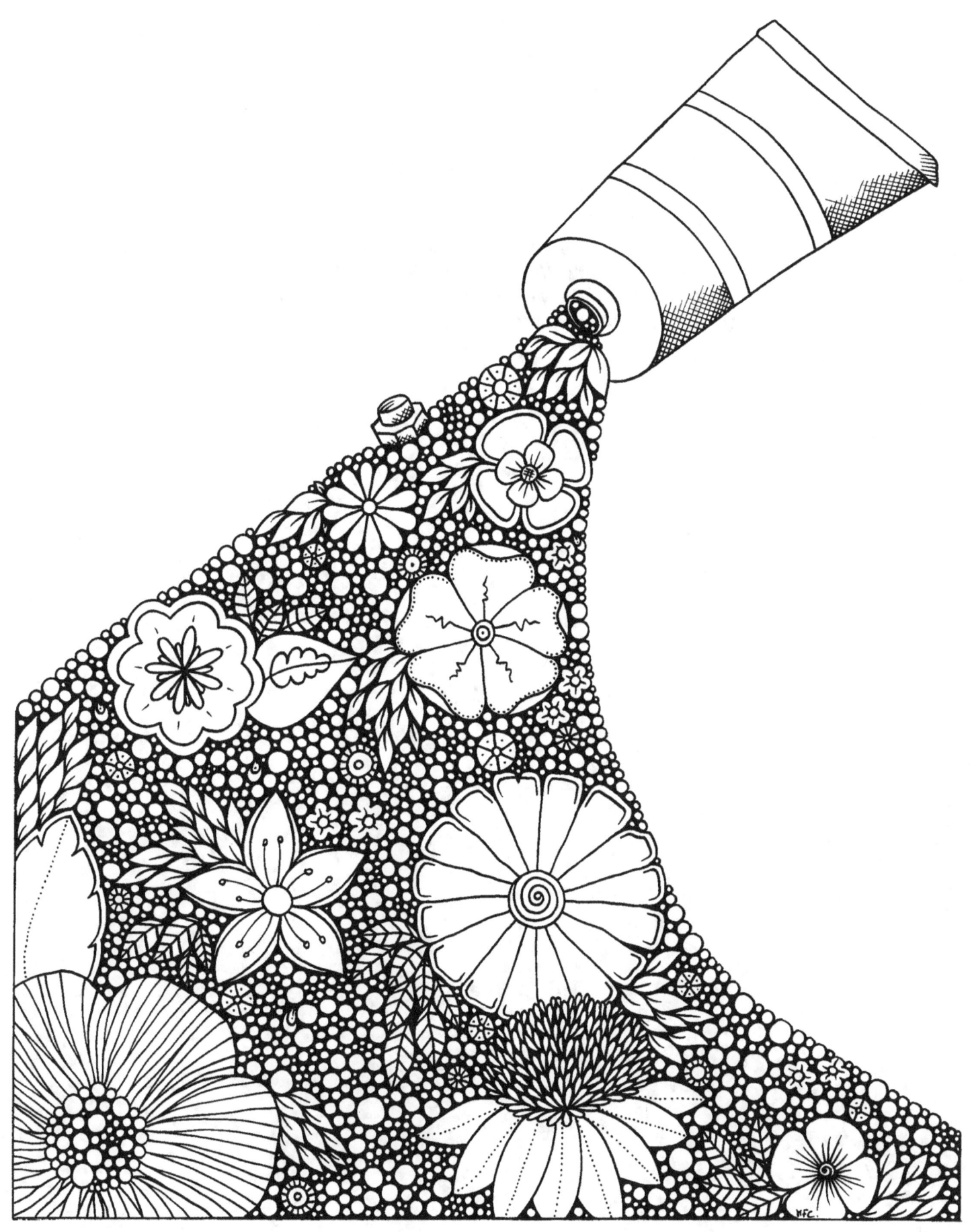

Contributing Artist
Maud Taron
France

Web : www.zendessin.com
Facebook : zendessin
YouTube : https://www.youtube.com/c/MaudT
Instagram : zendessin.maud
Pinterest : http://www.pinterest.com/taleque/
Shop : https://www.etsy.com/fr/shop/TalequeShop
More books : http://www.amazon.fr/Maud-Taron/e/B00QN8FGJS

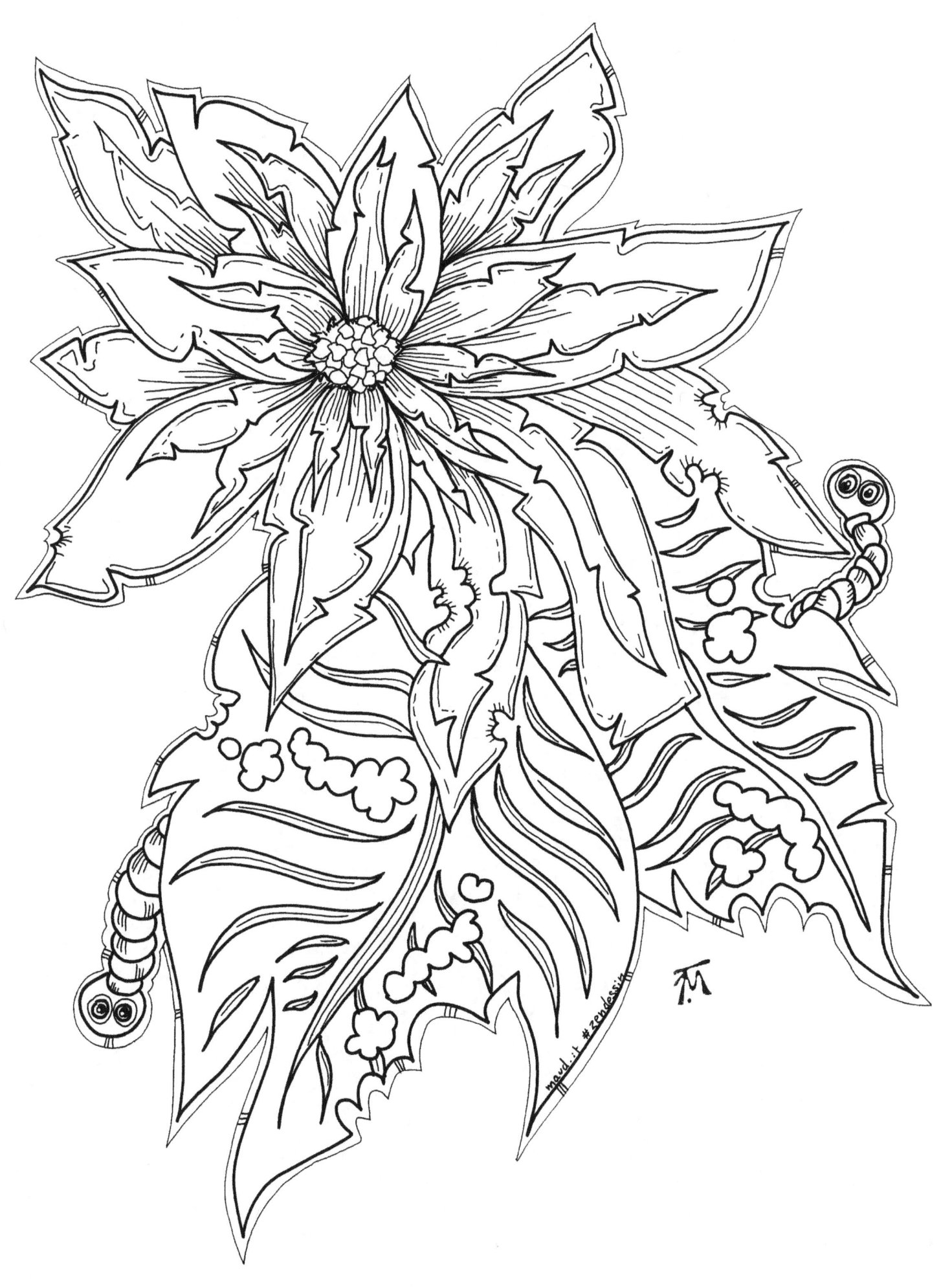

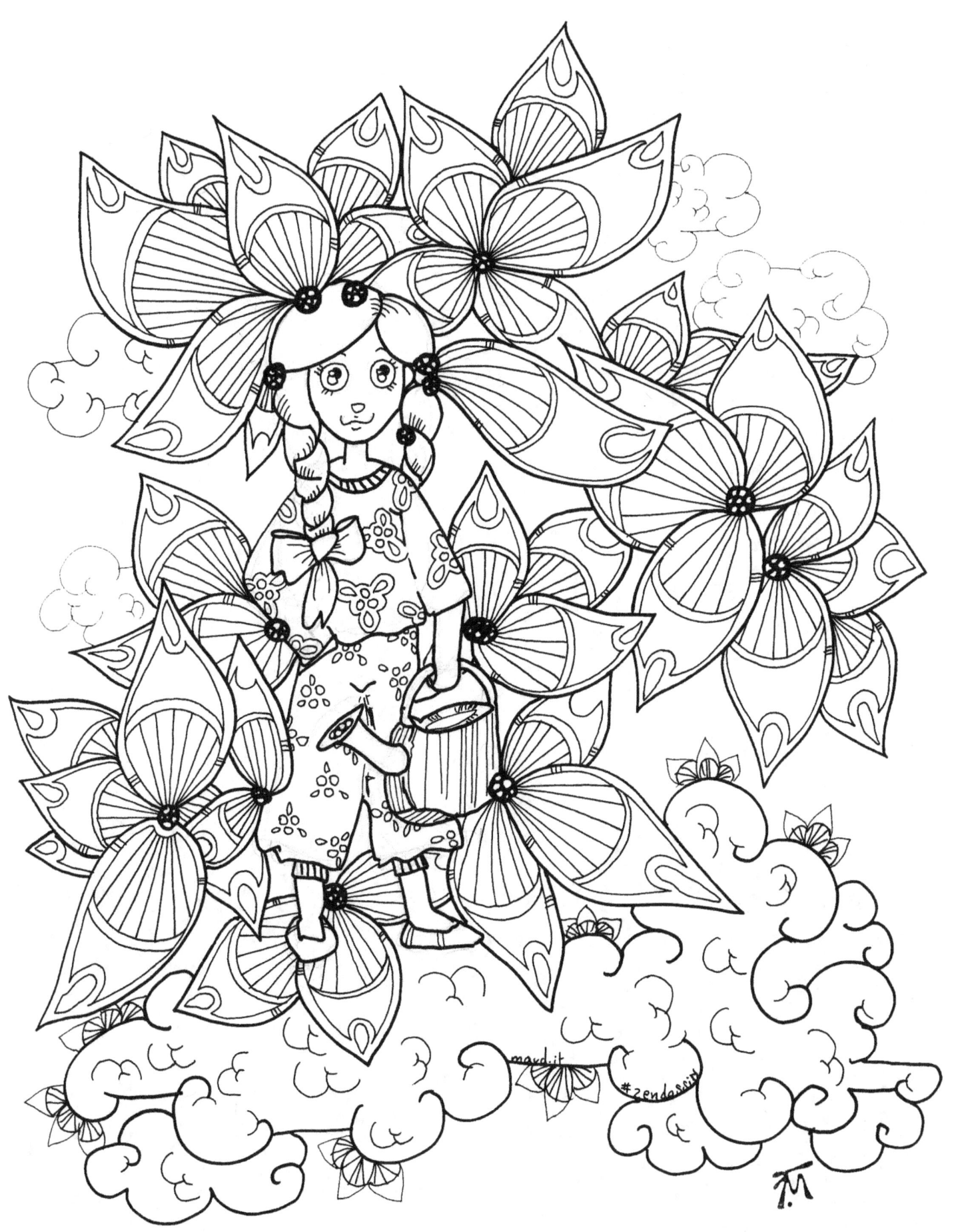

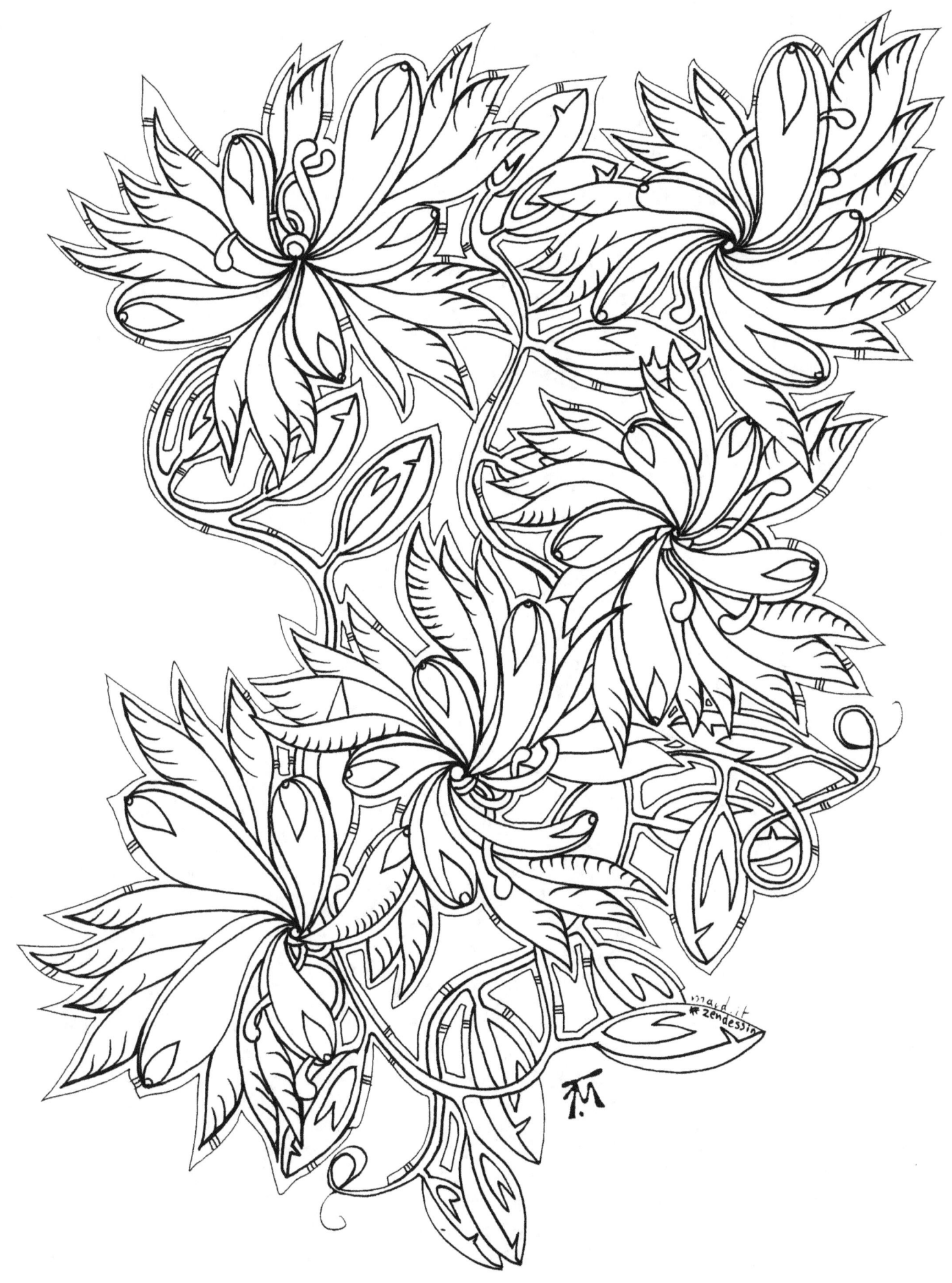

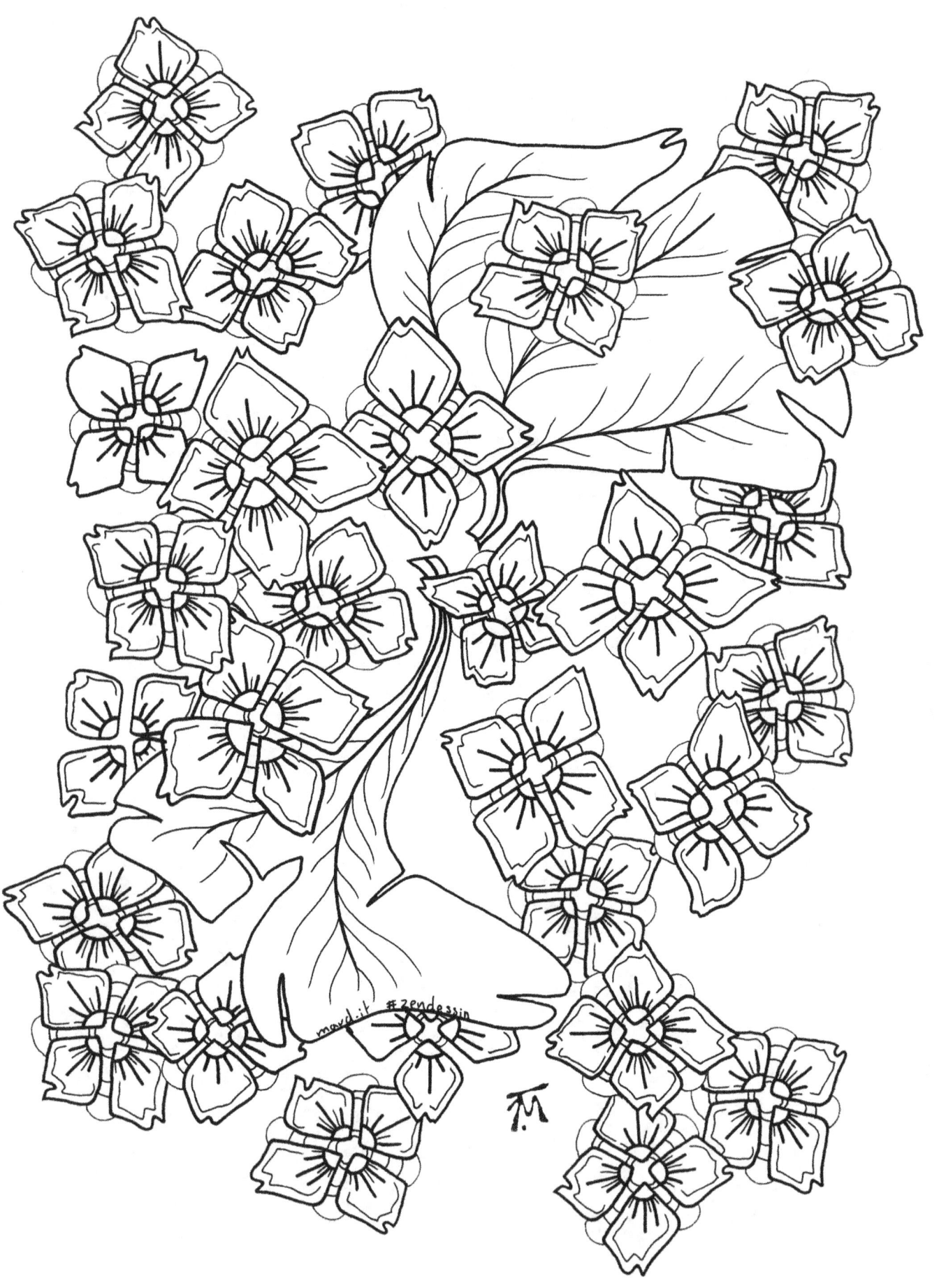

Contributing Artist
Isa Humeau
France

Facebook : graphizen

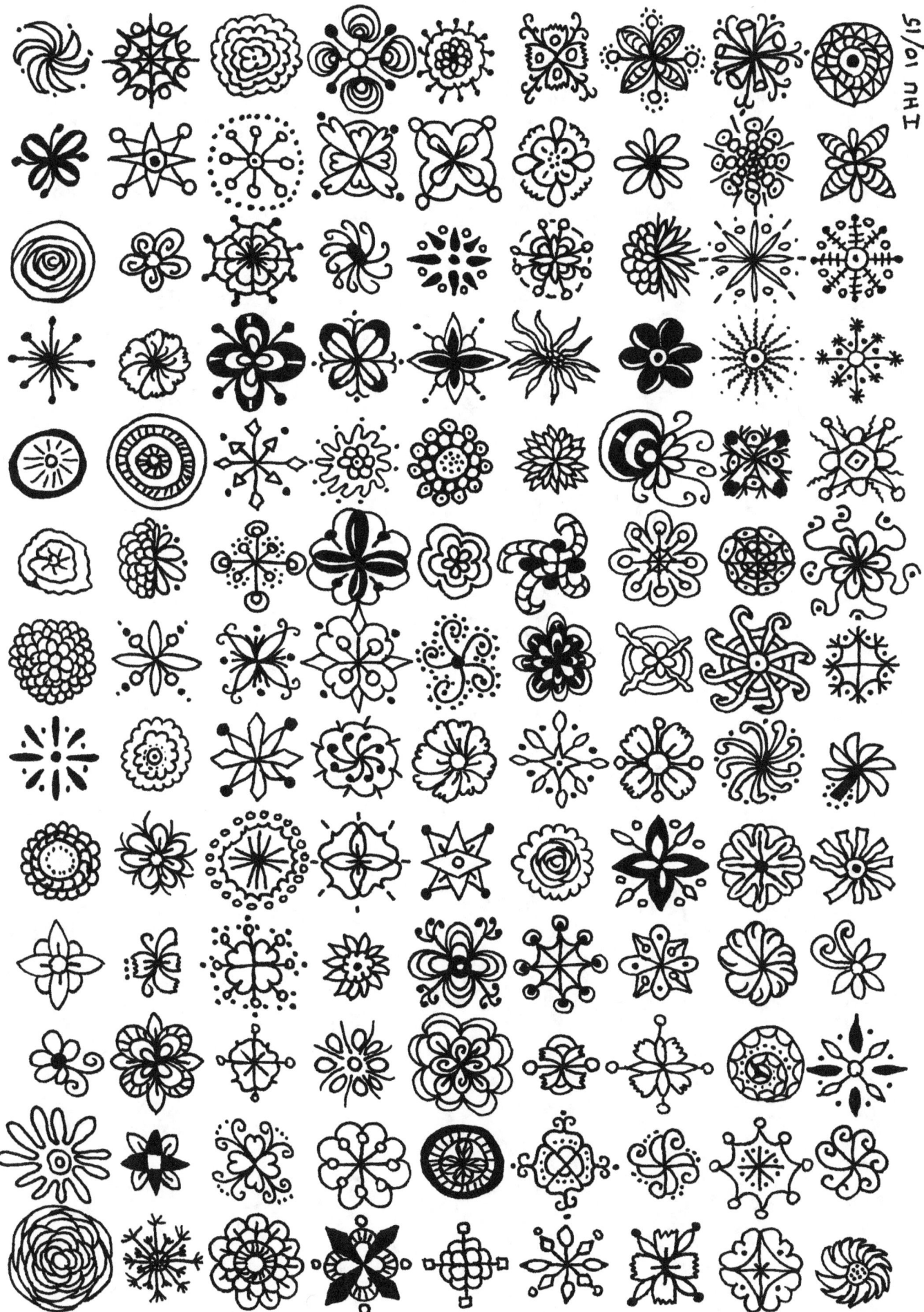

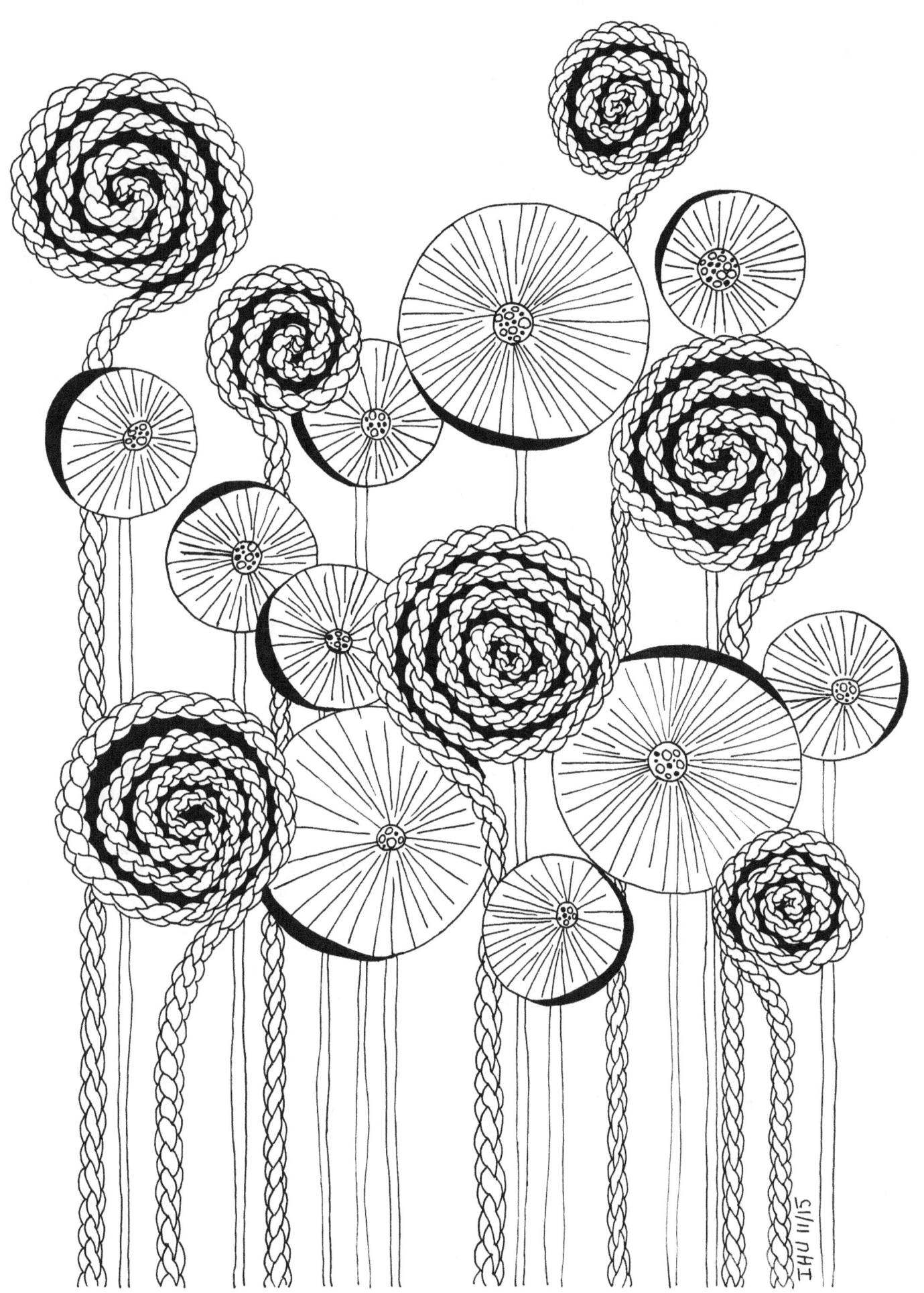

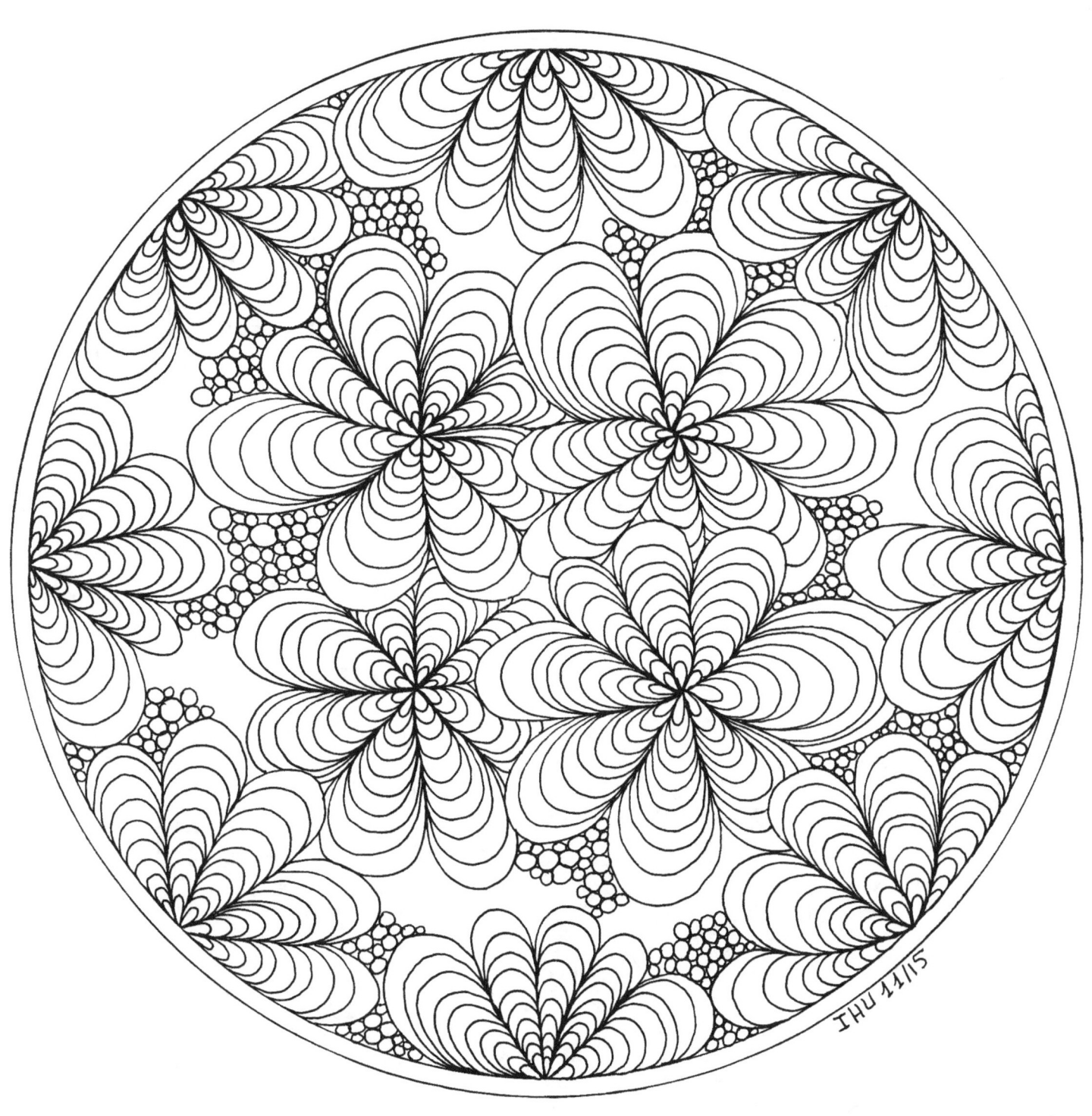

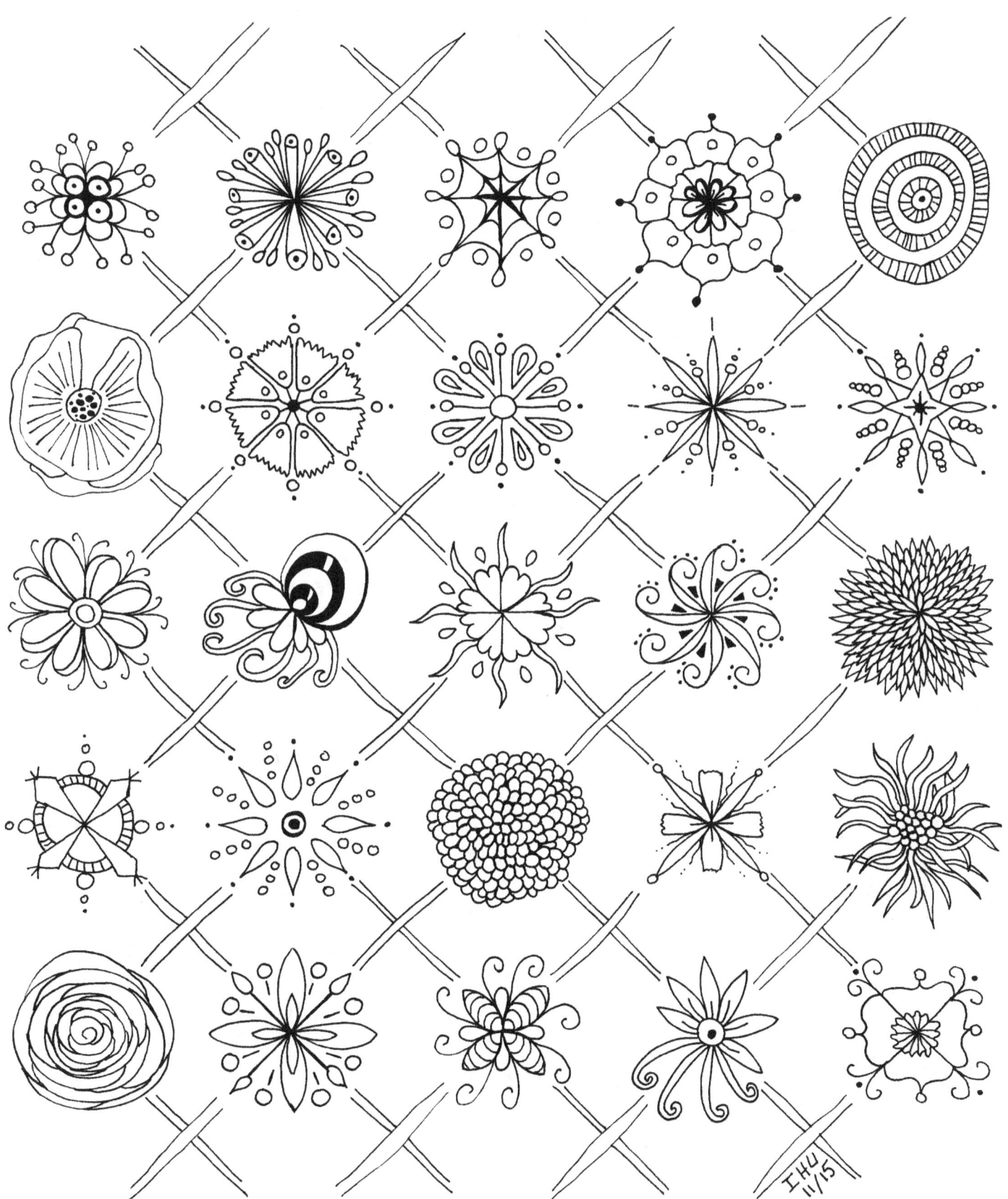

Drawn & colored by Lilan Chen	Drawn & colored by Mireille W	Drawn & colored by Nadege Zenfeerie
Drawn & colored by Rover Hsiao	Drawn & colored by Leaf Yeh	Drawn & colored by Neeti Goswami
Drawn by Yaya & colored by Vero Pignot	Drawn & colored by Johanna Ans	Drawn & colored by Ellen Wolters
Drawn & colored by Adriana Graciela Volpe	Drawn & colored by Alfred E. Villanueva	Drawn & colored by Maud Feral Chauveau (MFC)
Drawn & colored by Maud Taron	Drawn & colored by Isa Humeau	Drawn & colored by Nancy 43